PROVIDERS FINANCIAL INC.
2420 WEST VISTA WAY
SUITE 102
OCEANSIDE, CA. 92054

PROVIDERS FINANCIAL INC.
2420 WEST VISTA WAY
SUITE 102
OCEANSIDE, CA. 92054

Mortgage Banking
And Residential Real Estate Finance

By

The Masters of the Industry

Complied and Edited by
Patrick Mansell

Financial Advisory Press

Mortgage Banking
And Residential Real Estate Finance

by

The Masters of the Industry

Edited and Compiled by
Patrick Mansell

Financial Advisory Press is an imprint of:
Bimini Twist Adventures, Inc.
2911 NW 27th Ave.
Boca Raton, FL 33434
(561) 470-1279

ISBN 0-9728564-3-9

Cover Design by Paul Hammond- Studio 41, Boca Raton, FL

Manufactured in the United States of America

Contents

Foreward   xi

Introduction   *xiii*

Meet the Masters   *xvii*

Part I:
Mortgage Loan Programs   1

Custom Mortgage Financing - Dennis Kleinman   3

Conforming & Non-Conforming Loans
                           James Mansell   15

Alt-A Lending - Anne Hess Silver   23

Home Equity Loans - David Madison   31

Part II:
Know this Before Applying   **49**

Credit Reports and Credit Scoring - Alan Koch   **51**

Adjustable Rate Financing - Patrick Mansell   **57**

Loan Amortization - Patrick Mansell   **65**

The Role of the Commercial Bank in Mortgage Lending - Thom Bambenek   **73**

Part III:
Mortgage Handling   **79**

The Loan Application Process - Robert Lurer   **81**

The Closing Process - Marilyn Hevia   **95**

Borrower Beware! - Patrick Mansell   **107**

Mortgage Loan Servicing - Richard Higgins   **115**

Part IV:
Residential Real Estate   **123**

Valuation of Real Estate - Joel Greenberg   **125**

Building/Home Inspections - Bruce Sage   **143**

What Everyone Should Know about Mold - Bruce Sage   **155**

Part V:
Insurance Clearly Understood   163

Title Insurance - Peter Lopez   165

Homeowners Insurance - Maria Elena Cisneros   175

Private Mortgage Insurance - Don Rosenthal   187

Part VI:
Indispensable Tools for the Mortgage Banker
      205

Quality Control In Mortgage Originations -
James Hagan   207

Technology in Mortgage Originations -
Mac Russell   221

Valuing a Mortgage Company - Michael Henry   231

Glossary   255

Acknowledgments   269

FOREWARD

Each month for the better part of the last decade a small group of friends who are Mortgage Bankers, Mortgage Brokers and are otherwise related in one way or another to the Mortgage Banking profession, have had a standing dinner appointment. They meet, eat, drink, chat, and pretty much solve the problems of the world as they relate to lending money for the purchase or refinance of residential properties. They also tell jokes, sometimes smoke cigars, sometimes go to a baseball game or on gambling cruises, but it's all clean fun, and among them it really is quite possible to come up with solutions to most mortgage related issues. These guys know the business, are consummate professionals, and have the connections to make things happen. Euphemistically they refer to themselves as the South Florida Mortgage Braintrust, but I don't think any of them really believe they are members of any kind of think tank. We're just a bunch of friends who work in the same industry and chose to spend one evening each month together.

For several years I had given thought to the idea of writing a Mortgage Banking book that would unlock some of the mysteries of what goes on in a real estate finance transaction with respect to the Lender, and the steps he takes to protect the money he puts into the deal. Often home buyers and homeowners are agitated at the cost of such a transaction when all they want to do is put up their money and move into their house. Why is the mortgage company putting me through all this extra effort and expense? The fact is that there are perfectly logical explanations of what we do and why we do it.

So, at one of these Braintrust meetings I posed the idea that we collaborate on a book that would make sense of all this. I had written and published several books in the past and agreed that I would be the center of the effort. I would coordinate the editing, layout, graphics, and publishing. Enough of the members present at that meeting were warm to the idea and we began to move forward. But that only accounted for a half dozen articles, and that would not be enough to adequately handle the subjects we needed to cover. So we recruited from among our colleagues in the business who we also believed to be at the top of their industry and were authorities in a certain aspect of Mortgage Banking or related businesses.

The contributors for this book were selected because they are eminent professionals in their specialty. Few have less than twenty years of experience in their profession. Some have thirty years or more. Several contributors are Attorneys, others hold the titles of President and other high executive posts in public and private companies.

It's a good thing to have the knowledge and skill to navigate in the dynamic waters of Mortgage Banking. It's a much better thing to share that knowledge with others. And this book has been a pleasure, working with the contributors and watching so much experience and knowledge come together in one place to offer so much interesting and useful information.

INTRODUCTION

Mortgage Banking and Residential Real Estate Finance is a compilation of chapters written by professionals from the Mortgage Banking industry and related fields. With a view toward educating three potential target groups, home buyers, real estate finance professionals and students, these eighteen contributors set out to unlock, in plain English, the mysteries of the home financing process and the Mortgage Banking industry.

Many Mortgage Banking organizations are so vast that the job descriptions at the working level become extremely narrow. These firms have entire departments to handle, for example, collections. Within that collections area there might be ten specialists who handle only loans more than sixty days past due. How broad will the scope of knowledge normally be for a person in such a position? How could it be possible for this person to have a working understanding of title insurance, loan closings, credit scoring or real estate valuation? Now ask the question, "Would it be valuable for that person in the sixty days past due department to have a broader knowledge of the industry in which he or she works?" Wouldn't it even be better if that person simply had an improved understanding of how the servicing department, of which he or she is a part, works?

One of the things that makes the Mortgage Banking field so interesting is its diversity. Not only are there clerical jobs and management careers to be had, but there are also production, sales and organizational opportunities. In Mortgage Banking there is more money being moved around in a single day than in any other industry, save perhaps for the securities industry. This creates opportunities to specialize in the most sophisticated types of finance and analytics. This being the case, great minds can be challenged to do more, earn more, and be more creative. The topic of Mortgage Backed Securities alone congers up images of money markets on the local, national and international scale. The dollar volume of mortgage originations in the year 2002 exceeded $1.6 trillion. Then 2003 topped that. That's a market with legs! And *Mortgage Banking and Residential Real Estate Finance* is the book that can introduce people at all levels and of all interests to some of the more exciting and rewarding aspects of that business.

In addition to its appeal as a tool for Mortgage Banking organizations to educate their people, the contributors have made every effort to write at a level that a lay person can understand. To the vast majority of the general public, the purchase of a home is the single largest financial transaction they will ever make. Due to the intricacies and complicated nature of mortgage finance, it is not difficult to make an expensive mistake when entering into a home financing transaction. This book discusses every part of the loan transaction including closings, conforming verses non-conforming loans, title insurance, loan amortization, and a myriad of other related subjects. A home owner or home buyer can use this book as a guide to working his way through the financing transaction and learning the differences between adjustable rate loans, fixed rates, balloons, and home equity loans. In fact, it goes farther than just the financing transaction by also explaining in great detail home inspections, real estate valuations, title insurance and hazard insurance. These are all items and issues of great importance on which a prospective home buyer will spend a great deal of money. As opposed to making them mere expense hurdles a person must jump through in order to close on their purchase, this book makes them living topics which can provide critical information worth fortunes if used correctly.

What was once the domain of the Savings and Loan industry has more and more been taken over by the Government Sponsored Entities (GSEs) of Fannie Mae and Freddie Mac and the commercial banks. These large originators and servicers of mortgage loans are constantly inventing and perfecting new mortgage products. Commercial banks partner with Fannie Mae and Freddie Mac to securitize and sell billions of dollars of mortgage loans. This trade has grown to the point where many of the largest and strongest commercial banks do more residential lending than any other aspect of their business vis-a-vis Bank of America, Washington Mutual, Wells Fargo and Chase.

Today the Mortgage Banking industry is deeply rooted in high tech. We live in a world of artificial intelligence which is used extensively and successfully by Fannie Mae and Freddie Mac in their automated underwriting engines. A chapter in *Mortgage Banking and Residential Real Estate Finance* is titled *Technology in Mortgage Originations*. Many of the chapters discuss the Automated Underwriting (AU) engines of Fannie and Freddie and how they have simplified and sped up the mortgage process.

Of further interest to Mortgage Bankers and students is an article entitled *Quality Control in Mortgage Originations*. This chapter is an informative treatise for the professional Mortgage Banker that gives great insight into the means and methods lenders can and do employ to protect themselves against accidental and intended fraud. It provides real life, no-nonsense information, the kind that can be used by loan production department heads to help them identify critical weaknesses within their own organizations.

Because Mortgage Banking is such a diverse field and there are so many aspects of real estate related to it, it took 21 chapters on 21 completely different subjects to cover what need to be covered. This is a book that should be read from the front cover to the back cover only if the reader wants it that way. There's something for everyone and the book can be very useful in its parts. The home buyer who wants information on the correct procedure for having his contracted home inspected may not be ready or willing to read about the role of the commercial bank in real estate finance, but he would certainly want to read Bruce Sage's chapter on home inspections. Likewise, the CPA who needs to come up with a valuation for a client's Mortgage Servicing Rights might skip the chapter about how adjustable rate mortgages work, but would be very interested in Mike Henry's chapter, *Valuing a Mortgage Company*. In this book no one chapter is built upon any other so the reader is invited to approach the chapters the way that suits him or her best.

Mortgage Bankers, real estate professionals, homeowners and home buyers will profit by learning the lessons in *Mortgage Banking and Residential Real Estate Finance*. Nowhere else in literature today is this much practical knowledge about the industry, written by such knowledgeable and experienced professionals, available in one place.

Meet the Masters

James C. Hagan- *Quality Control in Mortgage Originations-* James Hagan received his undergraduate degree in Business Administration from Oklahoma State University, his JD from Oklahoma City University School of Law, and has been in mortgage lending since 1971. He is currently President of ADFITECH, Inc., founded in 1981, and is the leading out-source quality control provider to the mortgage industry. Prior to joining ADFITECH, he was President of ADFINET, Inc., and Oklahoma Mortgage Company, Inc., and has served as Director, Secretary, and General Counsel to the Oklahoma Mortgage Bankers Association.

Patrick Mansell- *Loan Amortization; Adjustable Rate Mortgages; Buyer Beware!-* Patrick Mansell entered the field of Mortgage Banking in 1969 after having earned a Bachelor of Business Administration degree from the University of Miami. Mr. Mansell is the co-owner of Coastal States Mortgage Corporation of Hollywood, Florida, which he co-founded in 1978. At Coastal States he has overall responsibility for mortgage originations, marketing, investor relations, servicing purchases and Quality Control. Before compiling *Mortgage Banking and Residential Real Estate Finance,* Mr. Mansell wrote and published six adventure novels. Mr. Mansell lives in Boca Raton, Florida.

Anne Hess Silver- *Alternative-A Lending-* Anne Hess Silver has been in the mortgage banking industry for many years in Florida and New York. She is currently employed by Impac Lending Group as a Regional Sales Manager, heading up a sales team originating wholesale mortgage loans from Mortgage Brokers in the Southeastern states.

Michael J. Henry- *Valuing a Mortgage Company-* Michael Henry is a Vice President in the Financial Institutions Group of Milestone Merchant Partners, LLC, where he specializes in merger and acquisition transactions involving mortgage companies and specialty finance firms. Prior to joining Milestone, Mr. Henry managed the analytics department of Bayview Financial Advisory Services. At Bayview he assisted in the analysis and execution of several corporate M&A transactions as well as managed the valuation of mortgage servicing rights. He received his Masters of Science in Finance from Boston College and his Bachelor of Business Administration degree from St. Bonaventure University. Mr. Henry also holds the designation of Chartered Financial Analyst.

Maria Elena Cisneros- *Homeowners' Insurance-* Maria Elena Cisneros was born in Havana, Cuba and came to the United States in 1961. She is a graduate of Barry University in Miami and is licensed in General Lines (Property & Casualty Insurance), Life, Health and Variable Annuity. In 1991 she began her association with State Farm Insurance Companies and is President of Cisneros Insurance Agency, Inc. offering insurance and financial services. She is a licensed Mortgage Broker, and holds a Series 6 license. During her career she has received numerous industry awards including the NALU National Sales Achievement Award, NAHU Leading Producers Roundtable President's Council Award, and has been a guest on national television and radio programs as an insurance professional.

David Madison- *Home Equity Lending-* David Madison is a divisional cross-sell manager for a major residential lender. Prior to this he was a top producing originator, funding over $250,000,000 in home mortgages from 1993 to 2000. Mr. Madison resides in Chapel Hill, North Carolina with his wife, Carol, and two sons, Alex and Dylan.

Dennis Kleinman- *Custom Mortgage Financing-* Dennis Kleinman received his Bachelors Degree in Marketing from the State University of New York at Albany. After completing a tour of active duty in the Army, he moved to Miami and attended Florida International University where he received a Masters Degree in Real Estate Finance. Mr. Kleinman has been involved in Real Estate and Mortgage Banking for over thirty years, having worked for Savings and Loans, Savings Banks and Mortgage Bankers. He has served as President of the Mortgage Bankers of Miami and has chaired a number of committees for the MBA of Florida. Currently Mr. Klienman is Senior Vice President of Residential Retail Lending at BankUnited FSB. His home is in Miami Shores, Florida where he lives with his wife Loretta and four sons, Seth, Danny, Michael and Andrew.

Mac Russell- *Technology in Mortgage Originations-* Mac Russell is President and founder of Russell Mortgage Network in Miami, Florida, and has originated over $400 million in residential loans. He has over 35 years experience in the mortgage, real estate and banking industries. Mr. Russell is a former Vice President for Citicorp Savings where he was the area manager for loan production, and where he was involved in the development of software used systemwide by the bank and by other large mortgage related companies. Mr. Russell was also Vice President of Residential Lending at Chase Federal. In 1990 he founded Russell Mortgage Network, a full service mortgage brokerage business. Mr. Russell is committed to the development of industry-specific computer technology to maximize the effectiveness of the company and its loan officers. He attended Duke University and the University of Miami. A life-long Miami resident, he enjoys music, photography and traveling through Florida with his wife, Janice. Mr. Russell can be reached by email at mac@russellmortgage.com.

Alan Koch- *Credit Reports and Credit Scoring-* Alan Koch is the Regional Sales Manager for CBA Information Services, a national credit reporting agency and Experian affiliate, headquartered in Cherry Hill, New Jersey. Mr. Koch has been with CBA since 1976. He has worked in many different departments within CBA including accounts receivable, Human Resources, property search and mortgage reporting. He is a member of the Mortgage Bankers Associations of Greater Miami and South Florida, the Florida Association of Mortgage Brokers and the National Association of Professional Mortgage Women. Mr. Koch lives in Boca Raton, Florida with his wife, Lyn and daughter, Shelby.

Bruce Sage- *Home/Building Inspections/Mold-* Bruce Sage is the Chief Operating Officer of Precise Residential Inspections, a residential, commercial, industrial and environmental inspection service in Coral Springs, Florida. Precise Residential Inspections provides inspection services to the consumer, real estate, legal and municipal sectors, and maintains contracts with the Florida Department of Management Services, Florida Department of Corrections, the Florida Department of Juvenile Justice and Building Code Administrative Services, Inc. Mr. Sage also serves as a FEMA international disaster housing project inspector and is the past Chair of the Coral Springs Code Enforcement Board. He has twelve years experience as a State of Florida Licensed Building Contractor, Construction Manager and Project Development Consultant, and has eight years experience as a Licensed Professional Building, Electrical, Mechanical and Plumbing Inspector. He is also a Certified Mold Inspector. A graduate of Rochester Institute of Technology (1971) and the U.S. Army Sergeants Major Academy (1995), Mr. Sage has served in the U.S. Army and Army Reserve for a total of 27 years and is the current Command Sergeant Major (CSM) of the 5th Brigade, 108th Division.

Marilyn Hevia- *The Closing Process-* Marilyn Hevia was born in Havana, Cuba in 1956 and traveled to the United States at a young age. After living in Pueblo, Colorado for three years, she has made South Florida her permanent home. She is fluent in both English and Spanish. Ms. Hevia is a management level executive with over 25 years experience in the financial field. She is currently Vice President of Production and Closing at Coastal States Mortgage Corporation where she has worked since 1983. After graduating from college in 1980 she pursued a career in mortgage finance, furthering her education with specialized course work. Ms. Hevia is professionally associated with the National Association of Mortgage Brokers, the Florida Association of Mortgage Brokers and the Mortgage Bankers Association of Florida.

Thom G. Bambenek- *The Role of the Commercial Bank in Mortgage Lending-* Thom Bambenek has been involved in commercial banking and real estate finance since 1972. After receiving his Bachelor of Science Degree from St. John's University he began his commercial banking career in South Florida. Mr. Bambenek spent sixteen years at SunTrust Bank as Senior Vice President of Real Estate Lending where he supervised the building of a high yielding portfolio of $1.2 billion in residential loans. In 2001 he joined Republic Bank as Senior Vice President of Residential Lending with responsibility for the entire southeast portion of the State of Florida. Mr. Bambenek is a member of the Mortgage Bankers Association of South Florida and is active in many community activities. He is a Board Member of the Juvenile Diabetes Foundation, President of Women in Distress, past Chairman and Board Member of Big Brothers and Big Sisters of Broward, and past Chairman and Board Member of the Academy of Finance. Mr. Bambenek lives in Davie, Florida with his wife Kathy and daughter Bridgett.

Joel B. Greenberg, SRPA- *Valuation of Residential Real Estate-* Joel Greenberg has been involved in residential real estate appraising since 1984. He has a Bachelor of Engineering Degree from Stevens Institute of Technology and holds the appraisal designation of SRPA. In 2000 Mr. Greenberg was asked to join a joint task force which was comprised of Fannie Mae, Freddie Mac, the State Comptroller's Office, FBI, Mortgage Bankers Association, Mortgage Broker's Association and the Appraisal Institute with a purpose of investigating mortgage fraud. He is also a Board Member of the Florida Quality Council, a professional organization dedicated to combating fraud in the mortgage industry, and is a Special Master for the Value Adjustment Board of Broward County, Florida. Mr. Greenberg is the President of Consolidated Appraisal and Research, Inc. of Coral Springs, Florida and can be reached by email at joelg@fdn.com.

Don Rosenthal- *Private Mortgage Insurance-* Don Rosenthal is the State Sales Manager in Florida for Republic Mortgage Insurance Company. He began his career in commercial real estate and has 25 years of experience in the residential mortgage industry with RMIC, during which time he has acquired vast knowledge in the area of loan production and default risk. When Mr. Rosenthal started his career in the mortgage industry there were only two mortgage insurance premium options, compared to the thousands there are today. He has worked with lenders to help borrowers obtain everything from affordable housing to mansions. Mr. Rosenthal attended Miami-Dade Community College and the University of Miami where he studied real estate finance. He is a member of the Mortgage Bankers Association of Florida, the Florida Association of Mortgage Brokers and the Association of Professional Mortgage Women.

Richard L. Higgins- *Mortgage Loan Servicing-* Richard Higgins has been associated with the mortgage banking industry since 1969 where he rose to the office of Vice President and Controller of a large nationwide mortgage banking firm. He holds the degree of Bachelor of Arts and is a graduate of the School of Mortgage Banking. In 1978 he co-founded Coastal States Mortgage Corporation, a full service mortgage lender, where he serves as its President. His responsibilities include mortgage originations, finance, mortgage servicing and investor relations.

Robert Lurer- *Retail Lending-* Robert Lurer is the founder and President of Continental Mortgage Services, Inc. of Plantation, Florida. He is a graduate of the University of Pittsburgh. With thirty-seven years in banking and lending, Mr. Lurer has held high level executive positions at several of the nations top lending institutions including BankAtlantic FSB, Metropolitan Mortgage Company/Transamerica, Gold Coast Savings Bank, Bankers National Bank and Chase Manhattan Bank. In addition to his vast lending experience Mr. Lurer has been a prominent force in various mortgage lending associations including Board Member of the Mortgage Bankers Association of Broward County, past President of the Florida Association of Mortgage Brokers, Board Member of the National Association of Mortgage Brokers, Advisory Board Member American Association of Mortgage Regulators, Member of the Single Family Lenders' Committee of the Mortgage Bankers Association of America. Mr. Lurer was appointed by the State Comptroller to a regulatory reform task force charged with the responsibility of rewriting the Mortgage Lending and Mortgage Brokerage law for the State of Florida.

Peter M. Lopez, Esq. - *Title Insurance-* Peter Lopez is a real estate attorney with the Law Office of Peter M. Lopez, PA, with over 12 years experience in commercial and residential real estate transactions. He has offices in Miami-Dade and Broward Counties, Florida, and his clients range from first time home buyers to commercial real estate investors. Prior to practicing law, Mr. Lopez was a licensed Real Estate Salesman and Mortgage Broker, which today enables him to give his clients valuable insight into the entire real estate transaction process. Mr. Lopez received his Bachelor of Arts degree in Finance from Florida International University and his J.D. from Florida State University College of Law. He is a member of the Real Estate, Probate and Trust Law Section, and the Entertainment and Sports Law Section of the Florida Bar. Mr. Lopez lives in Miramar, Florida with his wife Terry and sons Anthony and Peter.

Part I

Mortgage Loan Programs

Custom Mortgage Financing
by
Dennis Kleinman

When it comes to the financing of a home, compromise should not be part of a homeowner's vocabulary. A homeowner or home buyer should be prepared to take advantage of the many varieties of mortgage loans that are available today.

Mortgage financing was once no more complicated than choosing between vanilla and chocolate ice cream. Today's mortgage shopper can choose from many exotic flavors because creativity on the part of mortgage lenders has provided so many options to mirror the many different situations; the first time home buyer, the retiree, the wealthy professional and others. Today's mortgages are designed to help solve life's housing problems.

The Last Home a Person Will Ever Own

Ten, fifteen, twenty and thirty year fixed rate loans are as close to vanilla as it gets in today's mortgage market. The person who wants a loan that has set payments he can count on for the life of the loan would want one of these. Fixed rate loans have the same monthly payment of principal and interest over the life of the loan. Whether that loan is for ten years or thirty years, the payment remains the same until the loan is paid to maturity or paid off. It is important to know that when a loan fully amortizes, it pays itself off over the life of the loan. Each payment is composed of varying amounts of principal (the debt) and interest (the cost of borrowing). The amount that goes to principal and interest changes over the life of the loan, but the total principal and interest payment does not change.

3

For the person who wants to pay off his mortgage and own his home free and clear after a set period of time, this is the loan type for him. This loan is safe, secure and predictable but most often carries the highest interest rates.

Not Going to Be In The Home Too Long?

For the person who knows how long he is going to own a property, or if equity build up (debt reduction) is not a priority, and if the security of a predictable long-term interest rate is not important, there are lots of options available.

For example, intermediate ARMS of 3, 5, and 7 years have the stability of a fixed rate loan for their initial term and the thirty year amortization feature, but are priced more favorably. Thereafter they typically become a 1-year ARM. Their appeal is that they have the stability of payment coupled with low interest rates. Why pay for a long-term fixed rate loan if there is no intention of holding the property for that long?

There are other loan programs that allow a borrower to enjoy low interest rates such as balloon loans and interest only loans. A balloon loan offers the stability of a fixed rate loan for a finite period, say 5 or 7 years. During that time, the loan performs like a fixed rate mortgage in that monthly payments of principal and interest are applied. At the end of that period of time the entire loan balance is due. This loan is usually priced as low as or lower than an ARM, but it is critical that the borrower have a plan to handle the balloon payment at the end of the fixed term. The typical borrower is focused on having this property for less than the term of the balloon loan.

Interest only loans are gaining in popularity. They offer borrowers one of lowest payment streams. There is no required payment of principal in an interest only loan. What makes these loans so appealing is their resemblance to more mainstream mortgage loan programs. They may have a fixed payment period of 6 months to 10 years. During that time, the borrower has a minimum payment of the predetermined interest only. If he chooses, the borrower can make additional payments to reduce the principal, but that is not required. At the end of the fixed payment period, these loans become fully amortizing and perform like more traditional mortgages in their payment characteristics. Most interest only loans are based on the volatile LIBOR (London Interbank Offered Rate). This index rapidly and accurately shadows the movement of world interest rates. When rates are declining, this is great for the consumer. When rates begin to climb, consumers rapidly feel the effects in higher monthly payments.

Interest only loans are currently supplanting the previous champion of low payments, the deferred interest loan. The deferred interest loans (also known as negative amortization) have a payment amount that is not sufficient to meet the predetermined amortization schedule. This complicated loan program was very popular until the easier to understand interest only programs were introduced. The deferred interest loans may again come into prominence as savvy borrowers experience the effects of interest rate movements. Most deferred interest loans are based on the less volatile cost of funds index. This index moves more slowly than the Treasury index or LIBOR since it is composed of a bundle of savings instruments of various durations that are offered by financial institutions. There is a built in lag effect that benefits consumers when rates are increasing. However, when interest rates move in the opposite direction, downward movements are not felt as quickly.

Interest only loans are available as first mortgages and second mortgages. The most popular interest only second mortgage is the Home Equity Line of Credit, better known as a HELOC. There are a number of instances when a second mortgage is an important financing tool for a borrower. The interest rate on a HELOC is usually based on the prime rate. It allows a borrower to reserve a fixed amount of money that the borrower can access at any time, typically by use of a check or credit card. The appeal of the HELOC is that the borrower pays only for the amount of money accessed. This fund can be used, paid back and recycled multiple times, typically for the first 10 years of the loan.

Need a Low Down Payment?

There was once a time a borrower would need to put 20% or more into a property before he was able to obtain a mortgage. Today's borrower can get away with no down payment whatsoever. Somewhere in between is where the majority of home mortgages are being originated today.

The creation of the mortgage insurance industry, a revolution begun by the Mortgage Guaranty Insurance Corporation (MGIC), paved the way for borrowers to make down payments of less than 20% on the purchase of a home. The Private Mortgage Insurance (PMI) companies would insure a portion of the risk of default for the lender, while at the same time providing them with a mortgage with the same or better risk profile. For this service, the PMI company collects an insurance premium that was ultimately paid by the borrowers.

In this scenario the lender did not have to care if the borrower was putting down only 5% or 10% of their own money. The lender had the mortgage insurance to cover a portion of any loss suffered in a foreclosure sale should the borrower default. Today there are some PMI companies willing to insure a loan for upwards of 105% of the purchase price of the property. Today's borrower can choose from conventional and government low down payment loan programs. Both types of loans are offered by banks, savings banks, Mortgage Brokers and Mortgage Bankers.

The two direct government agencies that insure and guarantee mortgage loans are the Federal Housing Administration (FHA) and the

6

Veterans Administration (VA). The FHA insures both single family and multifamily residential mortgage loans. The VA guarantees mortgage loans given to qualified veterans. This FHA insurance and VA guarantee is in large measure what attracts capital into the residential mortgage market. A loan insured by FHA allows for a down payment of as little as 3%. In addition to that, it will allow the borrower to include closing costs in the loan. In a VA guaranteed transaction a qualified veteran can receive up to 100% financing.

Typically conventional loans require mortgage insurance to allow borrowers minimal down payments. However, there are loan programs that permit a conventional borrower to put down less than 20% and avoid the insurance premium that a private mortgage insurer requires. These "piggyback" mortgages are a combination of a first and second mortgages. Often the same lender offers them, but that not need be the case.

A piggyback loan is the combination of two mortgages that could total up to 100% of the purchase price of the property. This type of arrangement offers several advantages to the borrower. First, there is no private mortgage insurance premium to pay (private mortgage insurance premiums are not tax deductible). The interest on the second mortgage in most cases will be tax deductible and secondly, the combined payments of the two loans are frequently less than a single mortgage with a mortgage insurance premium. A Mortgage Banker, working in concert with an accountant, could advise the borrower which loan program is best for him.

Looking For The Best Cash Flow & Maximum Tax Advantage?

The maturity of the mortgage banking industry, as evidenced by the proliferation of various mortgage products, reacts to the needs of different borrower types. What was good for a conservative retiree might not be optimal for an aggressive younger couple seeking to purchase as much home as they possible can, or the well-healed borrower trying to maximize the tax benefits of home ownership.

For a home buyer to maximize his cash flow (enjoy the lowest monthly payments) there are a number of mortgage products. The aforementioned interest only loan is one, the deferred interest loan is another. In the case of the interest only loan, the borrower is not reducing his principal balance. In the case of the deferred interest loan, the borrower is actually adding to his balance but may have the lowest monthly payment of all. For example, consider the differences in monthly payments on the following loans. All loans are based on a $100,000 loan amount.

Loan Type	Interest Rate	Monthly Payment
30 Year Fixed	7.0%	$665.30
15 Year Fixed	6.5%	871.11
Interest Only	6.0%	500.00
Negative Amort.	1.5%	345.12

Another way to improve cash flow is to extend the amortization period of a loan. Although the typical maximum term of a mortgage is 30 years, some lenders offer terms of as long as 40 years. On the examples above, if the fixed rate loan became a 40-year loan, the payment would drop from $665.30 to $621.43. On the negative amortization loan the already low payment would decrease from $345.12 per month to $277.17. Although the savings may not appear dramatic on a $100,000 loan, consider the well-healed borrower with his $2,500,000 mortgage. With the negative amortization option, increasing the term from 30 to 40 years would change the monthly payment from $8628.01 to $6929.31, a difference of $1698.69 or nearly $20,400 in a year. This class of borrower frequently values cash flow over amortization.

The tax deductibility of residential interest payments is one of the greatest benefits of home ownership. Extending the term of the loan by increasing the number of years the borrower is paying interest can maximize these benefits. Interest only payments provide borrower with similar benefits because the entire monthly payment is income tax deductible and no portion of the payment goes to after tax principal. For those borrowers who are looking to maximize cash flow and the interest benefit that residential real estate provides, these are some of the best mortgage products available.

Stranger In A Strange Land

Home ownership is as American as apple pie, but ownership of real estate in the United States is not limited to only Americans. There are residents from many of the world's nations who recognize the value of owning property in the United States. These borrowers are typically lumped together and called "foreign national" borrowers. Here is a look at the typical foreign national borrower, as this buyer type is really composed of a number of different classes of borrowers.

Resident Aliens are people who have moved to the United States from another country and who have obtained formal residency status. They typically possess what is commonly called a "green card." This class of borrower is usually considered the same as American Citizens and is not treated like a foreign national.

Temporary Resident Aliens are usually here on a work or study visa. There are various visas that are issued by the United States for different reasons. Often, these borrowers are given the same rights and benefits accorded to American citizens when dealing with residential real estate.

True Foreign Nationals are people who are residents of another country who purchase second homes or investment properties in the United States. The documentation required of this class of borrower is different from that of U.S. citizens or resident aliens. Typically foreign nationals are required to put at least 20% of their own funds (equity) in a property and must verify assets in this country. There are various forms of alternative documentation that can be used to give lenders sufficient comfort to make a mortgage loan to a foreign national. America is still the land of opportunity. The ownership of real estate is open to the world so long as Mortgage Bankers find a way to provide financing.

Can't Verify Income or Assets?

There are four essentials that a mortgage banker looks for when considering making a mortgage loan. The value of the property as measured by an appraisal is just one factor. The three other factors relate directly to the borrower. These factors are credit, income and assets.

Lenders do not really want to foreclose on a home if the borrower does not make his payments in accordance to the terms of the loan agreement. They would rather the borrower make his payments in a timely manner. Indications of a borrower's ability and willingness to repay this loan are measured by their income and credit respectively. Specific guidelines are employed by Mortgage Bankers to measure the amount and quality of income. Income provides the borrower with the ability to repay a mortgage.

Credit reports are typically used to measure the borrower's likelihood of repaying the mortgage. If the borrower has a good track record of meeting his other credit obligations, he will likely display the same behavior in repaying his mortgage loan. A credit report also lists other monthly payment obligations that might impact the borrower's ability to meet the monthly mortgage obligation.

The last borrower component that is analyzed by mortgage underwriters is the liquid assets the borrower brings to the transaction.

If, for example, a borrower is making a 20% down payment on the purchase of a home, the lender wants to see that the borrower has this amount plus reserves available for the transactions. There are certain rules that govern what is considered qualified funds.

These rules, like the rules governing what qualifies as good income, good credit and good funds, are called underwriting guidelines. Underwriting guidelines differ from lender to lender and mortgage product to mortgage product. As noted herein, there are many mortgage products offered today. A product can be defined by its term, fixed rate or ARM, or by the guidelines under which it is originated. Since lenders like to view the four components of a mortgage loan in their entireties, those loans that give lenders the most information as to property, income, credit and assets are usually priced with the lowest interest rates and allow for the lowest down payments.

Loans that do not provide lenders with verification of some of these components are frequently called stated income loans, or stated income/stated asset loans, or no documentation loans. In the instance of a stated income loan, the applicant typically just states what his income is. The lender does not verify this amount. The stated income must be reasonable based on the profession of the borrower and his verifiable assets. Only the assets, credit and the value of the property are confirmed in this case.

With a stated income/stated asset loan, the borrower simply states what his income and assets are but is not required to verify either. Only the value of the property and the credit of the borrower are confirmed in this case. With a no-doc loan, neither the income nor the assets are listed on the application. The underwriter relies strictly on the value of the property and the creditworthiness of the borrower.

The loan programs with the least amount of documentation are priced higher than the fully documented loan programs. Why a borrower would pay more is based on their ability to meet the underwriting guidelines of the more fully documented loans. Not every borrower can meet the stringent documentation requirements of a fully documented loan, but they are no less credit worthy than those borrowers who can. These reduced documentation loans are another way the mortgage banking industry has met the needs of a diverse borrower universe.

When Does it Make Sense to Consider A Prepayment Penalty?

Recently pre-payment penalty pricing was introduced as a way a borrower can further reduce the interest rate on a mortgage loan. A prepayment penalty is a fee that a borrower must pay the lender for paying off their loan in a predetermined period of time. The typical prepayment penalty is for early payment in the first 3 to 5 years. Prepayment penalties can be a flat amount, like six months interest, or 2% of the outstanding loan balance prepaid in the first five years, or they could be based on a decreasing sliding scale of 3% of the outstanding principal balance in the first year, 2% in the second year and 1% in the third year.

A "soft" prepayment penalty is only charged if the borrower refinances with another lender. With a soft prepayment penalty there would be no penalty charged if the home is sold during the prepayment period. A "hard" prepayment penalty is charged regardless of the reason for the early prepayment.

For a borrower who is certain that he will be in his property for longer than the prepayment period, this could be a way to reduce his interest rate. Typically the difference between a loan with and without a prepayment penalty is .125%. Each borrower must weigh the risk versus benefit as they relate to his own situation. Again, the mortgage banking industry provides choices to potential borrowers.

Does It Make A Difference If the Property is Rented?

Occupancy of a residential property is generally divided into three categories: primary residence, second home or investment property. A primary residence is the place where the borrower lives most of the time. It is usually near the borrowers source of employment and what they generally call their home.

A second home is usually a vacation home. Underwriters will make certain that the purchaser of a second home is able to qualify for the mortgage payments without the use of rental income. If rental income is required to qualify for this property, it will likely be considered an investment property. Most lenders price a primary residence and a true second home the same with respect to interest rates and points. There are some underwriting guidelines for second homes that are slightly more conservative than those for a primary residence. Typically a second home owner can finance up to 90% of the value of a property while a primary homeowner can finance up to 105% of the value.

Investment property is typically purchased for rental income and equity appreciation. Most lenders charge a higher rate or higher costs when financing an investment property. Their logic is that there is greater risk of foreclosure when the residence is not the borrower's primary residence or home. Today an investor can purchase a residential property for up to 90% or more of the value of an investment property with the lender pricing for the greater risk.

Yes, the use of a property has a major influence on the pricing and underwriting of a mortgage loan.

Portfolio Loans

Underwriting guidelines are the rules that a lender uses to establish the eligibility of a borrower and a property for a mortgage loan. The foundation of modern underwriting guidelines is the so-called "Agency Guidelines." These are the underwriting guidelines that are used to originate loans that are targeted for sale to the Federal National Mortgage Association (FNMA) and the Federal Home Loan Mortgage Corporation (FHLMC). These guidelines take into account the financial loss experience these agencies have experienced on the loans that they have purchased from their contracted sellers. The underwriting guidelines are intended to limit or reduce the number of delinquencies or foreclosures on the mortgage loans they purchase.

Although millions of homeowners meet these agency guidelines and qualify for an agency loan, there are millions more who do not. This could be based on borrower type, loan size, income duration or amount, property size, or many other factors. For those borrowers who do not meet these agency guidelines, there are portfolio lenders.

A portfolio lender is one that originates mortgages as an investment and not for resale. Typical portfolio lenders are savings or commercial banks, insurance companies, pension funds, and credit unions which need an investment vehicle that mirrors the interest rate fluctuations of their liability accounts (CD's, savings accounts, insurance premiums, retirement benefits). Because portfolio lenders hold these mortgage loans for their own usage, they originate them with their own underwriting guidelines. Most often portfolio loans are not fixed rate mortgages. The typical portfolio loan is a short or medium duration ARM. Many of the more creative loans discussed earlier, interest only, deferred interest loans, and HELOCS are portfolio loans. Portfolio lenders also offer many of the no income qualifier loans discussed earlier.

There are many ways that the Mortgage Banking industry has created loan programs to meet the needs of nearly everyone who wishes to purchase residential property. The excitement is not over yet. As the needs of the home buying public changes, the mortgage banking industry will continue to evolve to meet those needs.

Conforming and Non-Conforming Loans
by
James Mansell

Conforming loans are defined as those loans that meet the purchase criteria of Fannie Mae and Freddie Mac as set forth in their Seller Servicer Guides. A broader definition includes the underwriting guidelines as established by the FHA (Federal Housing Administration) and VA (Veterans Administration). These two agencies of the US Government insure and guarantee mortgages that meet their own criteria, but they account for less than 5% of all new originations. For purposes of this discussion only the guidelines of Fannie Mae and Freddie Mac will be considered.

Conforming loans are recognized by many characteristics including size, term, borrower profile and property type. The guidelines for conforming loans are dynamic, meaning they change from time to time as conditions warrant. For example, in the 1980's the loan limits, meaning the largest dollar value of individual mortgages that Fannie Mae and Freddie Mac would purchase more than doubled from the low $30,000's to the high $60,000's. In the later part of the twentieth century that limit broke through $300,000 and continues to increase in response to increases in the cost of housing.

The world of conforming underwriting changed considerably with the introduction of AU (Automated Underwriting) which was introduced by Fannie Mae and Freddie Mac. Until the advent of AU lenders employed underwriters whose job was to examine loan files to see if they met the agencies' guidelines. Now computers do that job and the guidelines for loan approval have expanded considerably. There was a time when the guidelines specified that a borrower who made a down payment of 10% would qualify if he had reasonably good credit, adequate reserves, two years of continuous employment, and his housing payment to income ratio did not exceed 25%, and his total monthly payments, including housing and revolving credit, as a percentage of monthly income did not exceed 33%. This guideline was not cast in stone and there were areas where an underwriter could use a certain amount of discretion. For example, if this same borrower had many years of continuous employment and an exemplary credit record and vast reserves, the underwriter might be willing to approve higher payment ratios. Likewise if a borrower made a down payment of 20% and had good credit and reserves, the guidelines called for the underwriter to approve payment ratios of 28% and 36%. At the same time the underwriter had the flexibility to approve higher ratios under conditions where the borrower was exceptionally strong in the area of employment, credit or reserves. In this scenario the human aspect of underwriting could not be ignored. In spite of guidelines that were meant to offer flexibility in the determination of whether a loan was considered investment quality, many loan applications that met the conforming guidelines were not approved by underwriters, and many loans that did not meet the guidelines were approved. All too often the entire concept of whether or not a loan was a conforming loan was subject to human error or whim.

Many of the guidelines which underwriters in the past were supposed to follow have changed since the advent of AU. Years of research and many millions of dollars of software development have resulted in more flexible underwriting criteria and a more scientific approach to loan approvals. Today an underwriter, loan processor or loan officer can enter a loan application into Fannie Mae's underwriting engine called Desktop Underwriter (DU) or Desktop Originator (DO), or into Freddie Mac's Loan Prospector (LP) and receive an underwriting determination within a few minutes. Vast data banks with credit profiles and property values are accessed through AU.

Through the years of research done by Fannie Mae and Freddie

Mac in developing Automated Underwriting many of the past notions of what constitutes risk in a loan have been dispelled. For example, in the past the guidelines called for two years of verified employment, preferably in the same job, but at least in the same line of work. Since that time it has been discovered that job tenure is a weak indicator of risk in a loan, so under LP or DU an underwriter might expect a result that calls for income verification in the form of a previous year's W-2 or 1099, or a recent pay stub from an employer. Far less frequent is the requirement for two year's of full income tax returns, and almost never does a DU or LP result ask for business returns as was the case prior to the introduction of AU.

Emerging as the two most important elements of loan quality are credit scores and home equity. A borrower who is meticulous about his credit obligations resulting in high FICO or BEACON scores, in concert with the ability to make a sizeable down payment, is considered the strongest kind of borrower and approval for conforming financing is assured.

Guidelines for property have changed very little on account of AU, however, the requirements for appraisals has been dramatically affected. In purchase transactions the requirement for full appraisals with interior inspections remains the norm and is often handled differently than with refinance transactions. The underwriting engines use data banks of property values to set a range within which it is reasonable to expect a property value to fall. In fact, Fannie Mae and Freddie Mac's influence is so pervasive within the residential real estate community that a property submitted to AU has a strong likelihood of having been financed through one of those agencies some time in the past. Houseboats, condo hotels and time share properties remain ineligible.

The four most important considerations in loan underwriting simply stated are income, assets, credit and property. When all of these elements fall into their proper place the loan will qualify as a conforming loan and receive the designation 'investment quality'. Fannie Mae and Freddie Mac pool investment quality mortgages into securities called Mortgage Backed Securities which are bought and sold by investors of every kind. These high quality securities end up in pension plans, mutual funds, international portfolios and just about anywhere investments are made.

Securities backed by Fannie Mae and Freddie Mac are attractive for several reasons. The behavioral characteristics of conforming loans have proven over the years to have very low default rates which translates into a high level of performance. Additionally, Fannie Mae and Freddie Mac are two of the largest financial institutions in the world and their guarantee leaves little fear of loss of capital when investing in these securities. In fact, the quality of agency guaranteed Mortgage Backed Securities ranks second only to Treasury Securities which are backed by the full faith and credit of the United States Government. The lesson to remember here is that securities with strong backing will be more liquid and receive more favorable pricing in the investment market.

This brings up the issue of non-conforming loans. Loans can be non-conforming for many reasons and, as such, securities backed by this type of loan will be priced less favorably than Fannie Mae or Freddie Mac conforming Mortgage Backed Securities. Since the securities backed by non-conforming loans receive less favorable pricing, this inferior pricing must be passed on in the form of premiums charged to the borrower. Premiums in the form of higher interest rates and fees vary according to the degree by which a loan fails to meet the conforming standard. Further, some non-conforming loans cannot be securitized which will often result in still higher premium pricing.

None of this is meant to say that non-conforming loans are not good loans or that they are risky. Take the example of a very wealthy individual who has excellent income and credit and borrows $650,000 toward the purchase of a $2,000,000 home. The investor in this loan takes virtually no risk with respect to the possibility of default. With a very strong borrower and $1,350,000 in equity ahead of the loan, it would be very difficult for the lender to lose money on account of the borrower's failure to pay. On the other hand, this loan cannot be sold to Fannie Mae or Freddie Mac because the $650,000 loan balance exceeds their maximum loan limit. In this specific example there is still a market for the loan. Many institutional investors form their own securities and market them as alternatives to agency Mortgage Backed Securities. Since the loans in these securities are non-conforming and since they do not have the backing of one of the agencies, the securities will be less liquid and command a higher price. Some of the institutions backing these securities are very substantial and their backing of a security is considered to be quite strong. The higher price of the institutional backing verses Fannie Mae backing will be passed on to the borrower. Because the borrower in this example was well qualified and the loan was of exceptional quality, the premium charged will not be so great. In the same market where a thirty year fixed rate mortgage eligible for sale to Fannie Mae might be priced at 7.5%, this high quality non-conforming loan might carry a rate of 8% to 8.25%, or a premium of .50% to .75%.

The greater degree by which a loan deviates from the conforming standards, usually the higher the premium. In the example above, the only aspect of the loan that kept it from being agency eligible was its size. Other than that it was an excellent loan. But what about loans that are ineligible because the borrower is credit impaired? Or consider a loan where the borrower cannot verify his income or source of down payment. These situations are a bit further from the conforming standards and the premium a borrower will pay will be greater. There are issues of mortgage backed securities comprised of pools of loans of this type, but investors want a more significant premium in return for the risk they take. Default rates are generally higher for less than "A" credit borrowers and the collection efforts associated with this type of lending are much more extensive. In the market described above where a Fannie Mae fixed rate mortgage might be priced at 7.50%, a borrower who falls into this latter category may have to pay an interest rate of 9% or more.

There is another class of loans for which the secondary market is not well organized and for which there is very little liquidity. Loans to foreign nationals and to corporations, both domestic and foreign, and loans on condo hotel and time share units are generally ineligible for purchase by Fannie Mae and Freddie Mac, and have not been well accepted in the Mortgage Backed Securities of traditional institutional investors. Due to this illiquidity, the market for loans of this type is limited to institutions that are willing to hold them as whole loans in their own investment portfolios. Often it is the local commercial bank that makes this type of loan and their motivation and philosophy of lending is much different than it would be for an institutional investor. For one thing, most commercial banks that are regulated by the Office of the Comptroller of the Currency (OCC), or Savings Banks that are regulated by the Office of Thrift Supervision (OTS) are, in general, limited with respect to the maximum term for which they can lock in a rate. Therefore, fixed rate financing would probably not be offered. Further, such a bank would be inclined to look for other areas of safety in the loan itself, such as lower loan-to-value ratios and additional personal guarantees.

Loans of this type are from time to time sold between banks, but the pricing is not very competitive and the market is limited. For all these reasons, loans that fit into this category can expect to carry a much greater premium for financing. Since these loans are most often limited to adjustable rate financing, a comparison to Fannie Mae adjustable rate financing would be appropriate. Where the market rate for a Fannie Mae conforming five year ARM might be 5.0%, a foreign national or corporate borrower could expect to pay a rate of 7.0% for the same loan.

In general, the farther from the conforming norm a loan is, the less liquid is the market for that loan. The most liquidity in the mortgage market comes from Fannie Mae and Freddie Mac Mortgage Backed Securities which are populated by conforming loans and these loans command the best prices. Conversely, the farther from the conforming norm a loan is, the higher the price will be.

Alternative-A Lending
by
Anne Hess Silver

In the early to mid 1990's a new product emerged in the mortgage industry. It was a loan based solely on the credit of the borrower and the collateral, with income and assets "not verified". This product was known as the "NINA" (no income, no asset) loan. The mortgage lenders who specialized in this product became known as "ALTERNATIVE A" lenders, later shortened to "ALT-A".

Since 1999, many billions of dollars of Alt-A securities have been issued. Investor acceptance of, and demand for Alt-A securities has been fueled by the participation of Fannie Mae and Freddy Mac in this sector. In the past, investors in these securities relied almost universally on the credit score ranges contained in the mortgage pool as the indicator of expected performance. As the growth of this market continues, characteristics of the securities have broadened. Investors must now look at a range of factors to determine minimum risk. These include:

1. The types of collateral: single family residences, 2-4 unit properties, garden condos and high rise condos, planned unit developments (PUDs);
2. Occupancy types: owner occupied, second homes and investment properties;
3. Product type: fixed rates, arms, balloons; interest-only options;
4. Purpose: purchase or refinance loans;
5. Loan size;
6. The presence or absence of prepayment penalties;
7. Loan to value: from 100% and below.

Types of 'Alternative-A' loans have also evolved. Where once the product was only a 'no income' verification loan, a true 'NINA' emerged. Eventually certain lenders offered a complete 'No Doc' loan, which required no employment, no income and no asset verification. Hybrids later developed. 'No Doc with verified assets' means that no employment information or income is provided, but assets are verified. 'LISA' loans are loans that contain 'light' income verification and 'stated' assets. Documentation for this type of loan is typically twelve months of personal bank statements (or twelve months of business bank statements if the borrower is self-employed) and stated, not verified, assets to close. Another hybrid is known as the 'FISA' loan, full, verified income with stated, not verified assets. Pricing of these loan types varies depending upon the perceived amount of risk. Loans that contain more verification are priced more favorably than loans with little or no information verified such as No Doc.

Alternative-A mortgage securitizations are analyzed and rated by a number of factors, including product with different levels of documentation, different property types, credit score ranges, mixed amortization types, varying repayment terms, loan size and geographic distribution of collateral. Performance characteristics of the securities is measured by delinquency, default, prepayment behavior, loss severity and cumulative losses. Interest in these securities expands as investors begin to have a better understanding of expected performance.

Who is the Alt-A Borrower?

Traditionally ALT-A borrowers are A-credit rated, but associated with characteristics that make them ineligible for traditional conforming or agency (Fannie Mae, Freddie Mac, FHA and VA) lending programs.

Credit

Since income and assets are typically not supported, credit

history and depth are important indicators of the borrower's ability and willingness to repay debt. In most Alt-A underwriting, lenders are looking for at least two years history of managing credit successfully and having a least five trade lines reported by the credit agencies. Another important indicator is having current housing expense. The manner in which a borrower pays his current rent or mortgage is considered a strong indicator of how he/she will handle the new mortgage payment.

The underlying credit quality of a borrower is typically measured by his credit score. Although there can be a wide range of credit score "buckets" in the Alt-A lending programs (i.e.580 and above) most borrowers have A rated credit (640 and up). There is a strong correlation between credit scores and permissible loan to value ratios. Generally the higher the score, the more credit worthy the borrower is, and the higher the permissible loan to value.

Not only is depth of credit and credit score considered, but also late payments or delinquencies will be taken into consideration. For example, most Alt-A lenders look at the mortgage or rental history for the past twelve to twenty-four months. At certain higher LTVs, there can be no late payments reported on the mortgage account within the past twelve months. Generally speaking however, late payments on consumer credit, installment and revolving loans, will not be considered in the credit grade at LTVs of 90% or lower. Judgments, collections, charge-offs, repossessions, and other credit related liens can be indications of serious problems and applicants with items such as these on their credit reports will not fit into Alt-A or conventional underwriting guidelines. An exception to this policy would be medical collections, however these usually must be paid off at closing. Bankruptcies and mortgage foreclosures generally follow conventional underwriting guidelines which state that the borrower can not have had a bankruptcy in the past two years or a foreclosure within the past three years.

Assets:

Under conventional underwriting guidelines, the borrower is expected to prove that he has the funds available for the down payment, closing costs and reserves. A NINA borrower is not required to verify the cash needed to complete the transaction. Instead, simply "stating" required assets on the mortgage application, or leaving the assets section of the loan application blank, will be sufficient.

Employment:

While income is not verified on Alt-A loans, employment is verified. Lenders offer loan programs for salaried, self-employed, and retired individuals. In some cases lenders offer a NO DOC loan wherein employment is not even required to be stated. Guidelines vary, but typically lenders require two years of employment in the same line of work if salaried, or two years in the same job if self-employed. Underwriters will take into consideration an individual who has perhaps just finished college with a degree and is starting to work in a professional capacity. Therefore, a borrower who has just a few short months on a job may be eligible for a NINA loan if he can prove that he has been preparing for this position in college.

Risk Based Underwriting.

Alternative-A loans are underwritten utilizing a "risk based" approach. Because levels of documentation vary, the essential requirement of prudent underwriting is that the terms of the loan be directly related to the borrower's probability of repayment and the value and marketability of the mortgage collateral. This is unlike conventional underwriting which is based on credit ratio requirements for housing expense and other total debt to income ratios, and where repayment can be predicted in a more precise manner. In these loans, employment, income, and assets are verified and clearly known to the underwriter.

26

Because of the various levels of documentation and verification in Alt-A underwriting, loan characteristics tend to be directly related to one another. For example, a borrower who has a high credit score will likely be granted a higher loan to value than a borrower with a lower score. A property that can be compared with very similar properties to determine market value, as opposed to a property requiring large adjustments due to dissimilarities, will allow for a higher loan to value. If two borrowers have similar credit scores, but one borrower can verify assets and the other cannot, the verified assets loan will be looked upon more favorably. Not only will a higher loan to value be considered, but the loan amount could also be higher.

Alt-A underwriters will often refer to "layers of risk." Typically each layer of risk will be met with a pricing "add-on." For example, a low credit score may be given a 25 basis point price adjustment. A high loan to value may be given another 25 basis point adjustment. Investor properties, as opposed to owner-occupied properties, will likewise be adjusted. Each "layer" of risk (low score, high loan to value, non-owner occupied properties) is subject to a pricing adjustment to compensate the lender for the increased risk.

Alternative-A Case Scenarios

Here are a few typical scenarios where a borrower would be a candidate for an Alt-A loan.

Case # 1:

Bob Smith has been a waiter for five years. In this time he has worked for three different restaurants, with no time off between jobs. Since the largest part of his income is from tips, of which only a portion is reported, he does not have an acceptable debt to income ratio based upon verifiable income. Bob has rented in the same apartment complex for the last three years and pays monthly rent of $800. He has always paid rent on time and the lender will be able to obtain an excellent verification of rent from his landlord.

Bob has found a condo that he wishes to purchase for $150,000. He has a bank account totaling $5,000 and knows that his father has promised a gift of $20,000 to purchase a home. Bob also keeps cash in his apartment of approximately $2,000, so he knows he will have enough funds to purchase the home, but he cannot verify that all the funds needed to close are 'seasoned' in the bank.

In addition to paying his rent on time each month, he has maintained good credit for several years, with the exception of a 30-day late on his car loan several months ago. He has 6 trade lines on his credit report and a credit score of 651.

Bob makes a mortgage application with his mortgage broker for a 95% loan. His broker advises him that he needs to consider a NINA loan because he cannot verify his income or his assets. On the loan application no income is stated and assets are "stated" $27,000. The loan is approved with an Alt-A lender. His credit score of 651 qualifies for 95% financing. The one time late payment on his installment is overlooked because of his good overall credit.

Case #2

Sally Score is a schoolteacher, working at the same school for four years. She has been living with her fiancé for the last two years in an apartment that they rent. Sally has excellent credit with a score of 695 and has six years of strong credit history with many trade lines and very few consumer credit late payments. She and her fiancé wish to purchase a home valued at $350,000. Her fiancé has an excellent job and a high income and can easily afford the mortgage payments but has had credit problems in the past and has very low credit scores. There is no way that he can be a co-borrower on this loan. They wish to put down 10% and most of the down payment is in the fiancé's bank account. They will both occupy the new home qualifying them both as owner occupants for underwriting purposes.

Sally makes an application with her mortgage broker, explaining the details of her situation. The mortgage broker suggests a NINA loan, with Sally as the only borrower. In this case, although the employment is verified, the income section of the loan application is left blank, because if income were stated, it would have to 'make sense' or be reasonable. Generally it would not be deemed reasonable to think a teacher could support a mortgage loan in the amount of $315,000. The approval of credit will be based solely on her score. Additionally, assets are stated, not verified. The lender approves the loan and Sally and her fiancé move into their new home.

Case #3

Charles and Barb have owned a hair salon in New York for many years and have a strong client base and a very successful business. They have managed to save over $250,000 and decide that they would like to move to a warmer climate. They sell their home in New York and move to Miami, Florida. Because they are so knowledgeable in the salon business, they rent space in a very chic area of Miami Beach and set up a beautiful salon. They find a home they wish to purchase and go to a local mortgage broker to obtain a mortgage.

Charles and Barb each have excellent credit scores, well above 700, and they have ample funds for a 10% down payment. Because they have years in the same line of work they anticipate no problems obtaining a loan. However, their mortgage broker sees the situation differently. True, they have been successful, self-employed salon owners for many years, but a salon is strictly a client-based business, and being new to the area they do not have an established client base that will provide a stable income stream. The broker suggests a "No Doc with verified assets." They are approved for the mortgage and close on their new home.

The philosophy behind an Alt-A loan is that there is a loan for every borrower. Alt-A lending is not sub-prime lending, but rather, lending that offers alternatives to "conventional" guidelines. This is a very big distinction in the respect that sub-prime loans are priced to take into account the added risk of lending to borrowers who may have a higher propensity to default. Alt-A borrowers have proven their willingness to repay their loan obligations over time which translates into much better pricing for them.

Home Equity Lending
by
David Madison

Home Equity financing is perhaps the fastest growing area within residential mortgage lending. It is a profitable category of business for mortgage lenders, an important product set for loan originators, and a class of loans beneficial to many homeowners in various circumstances.

Home Equity loans and lines of credit are prized as sources of loan funds, often considered preferable to automobile loans, credit cards, student loans, store charge accounts, and other forms of unsecured debt. That is because Home Equity products frequently are priced by lenders at lower interest rates than these other forms of debt, and for most borrowers under most circumstances the interest on Home Equity loans and lines of credit is tax deductible.

A homeowner can arrange for a Home Equity loan when acquiring the property or afterwards, when he already possesses the property. Home Equity financing usually, but not always, appears as a subordinate lien on a home. That's why the term "second mortgage" is often used synonymously with the term "home equity loan."

When there is a first mortgage in place, that lien has legal priority over the claim of the Home Equity lender in the event of default or foreclosure. Before the Home Equity lender can recoup its loan funds if there is a foreclosure, the first lender's debt must be satisfied. Proceeds from the sale of the home first go to repaying that loan balance, plus accrued interest, fees, and costs of collection. There frequently is little or even nothing left to repay the Home Equity lender. That makes Home Equity lending more risky than traditional first mortgage lending, which explains why rates are often higher on Home Equity financing than first mortgage loans.

Product Types

Home Equity mortgages fall into one of two types, although in recent years we have seen hybrids of the two. The first general type is the Home Equity Line of Credit (also sometime called a "HELOC"). This is the most popular Home Equity product, especially when short-term interest rates are low. Lines of credit are set up as revolving facilities, similar in nature to credit cards. During the initial, or draw-down period of the loan, the borrower has access to the line or credit. Borrowers may draw down, or borrow, all or a portion of the available line of credit. Each month they are required to pay the accrued interest. Depending upon the lender's terms and conditions, the borrower may also be required to pay down a portion of the outstanding balance. The borrower may continue to draw down and repay all or a portion of the available line, borrowing and repaying funds over and over again. Once the access, or draw-down period has expired, the borrower is required to repay the balance of the loan over the remaining loan term. The total term of the line of credit may range typically from five to thirty years, with the draw-down period usually lasting five to ten years.

The interest rate on most lines of credit is based on a known index such as the Prime Rate ("Prime"). Some lenders use LIBOR (London Interbank Offered Rate), Treasury bill rates, or perhaps other indices, but the vast majority of lines are based upon Prime. A margin over or below the index is then added or subtracted, and that determines the rate. For example, if Prime is at six percent, and the loan note indicates that the rate is Prime plus 1%, the borrower's rate is therefore 7%. Most lines of credit have variable rates, meaning that as the index moves up or down, the borrower's rate moves accordingly. That can have an impact on the borrower's monthly payment, both during the draw-down period and the repayment portion of the loan term. Some lenders establish floors and/or ceilings or caps, below or above which the rate cannot move.

The second broad category of Home Equity product is the fixed rate loan. These work in similar fashion to traditional fixed rate first mortgages. The lender funds the entire balance of the loan at the beginning of the loan term, and the borrower repays the debt in fixed monthly installments based upon an amortization schedule. The amortization schedules generally range from five to thirty years, and the loans may be fully amortizing, which means the amortization period and the loan term are identical. Or, the loan term could be shorter than the amortization period, which means that the remaining balance of the loan is due to be fully repaid on or before a specific date. This would create a balloon payment.

As previously mentioned, a limited number of lenders are offering hybrid products combining features of both lines of credit and fixed rate loans. One such example allows the borrower to utilize their mortgage as a line of credit for a certain period of time. After the expiration of this first portion of the loan term, the loan balance is then repaid based upon a fixed rate with fixed payments for the remainder of the loan term.

Both credit lines and fixed rate loans have their advantages and disadvantages. The loan officer and borrower must evaluate the borrower's circumstances, needs, and risk tolerance, and then match them up with the Home Equity product that has the most appropriate terms and conditions.

Lines of Credit

Advantages
- Repeated access to funds, even after the line has been repaid;
- Monthly payments based only on the outstanding balance,

and, depending upon the lender's terms, perhaps an interest-only payment;

- Low interest rates when the indices used are at low levels.

Disadvantages
- Variable interest rates can move up appreciably;
- Payments are not fixed, making monthly budgeting potentially more difficult;
- Either no requirement or minimal requirement for repaying principal during the access period. A borrower may use the credit line to purchase an asset, such as an automobile, and then fail to make adequate principal reduction payments. The result a few years later could be that the borrower owns a car that has limited value while the additional debt on the home could be for the original purchase price of the vehicle. Or worse, the homeowner no longer owns the car, having sold or traded it, but still has the debt on the home; and
- Temptation to access funds for inappropriate purposes, such as day-to-day living expenses, stripping the borrower's accumulated equity in the property.

Loans

Advantages
- Fixed rate of interest;
- Fixed monthly payments, making budgeting easier, and reducing the need for discipline in properly paying down the principal balance. Keep in mind that if a Home Equity loan is used to acquire a shorter-lived asset than the term of the mortgage, the borrower still runs the risk of having a debt on the home greater in amount than the value of the asset; and
- No temptation to borrow additional funds after closing for inappropriate uses.

Disadvantages
- When short-term interest rates are low, the interest rates on Home Equity loans can exceed the rate on lines of credit;
- No further access to loan funds once the loan has been paid down; and
- When the loan balance has been paid down appreciably, the required monthly payment is typically significantly higher than the required payment for a line of credit with a similar outstanding balance.

When and Why are Home Equity Lines and Loans Used?

Home Equity mortgages are obtained at one of three times. The first is when the property is being acquired by the homeowner. Second, when the homeowner refinances the first mortgage on the property. The third possibility is some time thereafter, when the borrower already owns the home, has some equity in the property, and wishes to utilize this equity as collateral to obtain funds either for reserve purposes or some other specific use.

When placed on the property at time of acquisition or first mortgage refinance and behind a traditional first mortgage, the Home Equity financing is frequently referred to as "piggyback" financing. Let's take a look at the primary reasons why a home buyer might want to obtain a HELOC or Home Equity loan at the time the property is bought or being refinanced.

Eliminating the Need for Mortgage Insurance

Generally speaking, whenever a home buyer obtains a home and puts down less than twenty percent of the purchase price of the home, the lender requires that the borrower pay for Private Mortgage Insurance ("PMI" or "MI"). This insurance coverage protects the lender in the event of borrower default, repaying the lender a portion of the loan amount if the lender loses money after gaining possession and then selling the property. The insurance premium typically ranges from approximately ¼% to ¾% of the loan amount per year, usually payable on a monthly basis along with the borrower's principal and interest payments.

Many lenders waive the PMI requirement for borrowers putting down less than twenty percent if the first mortgage is not greater than eighty percent, with all or a portion of the remaining funds needed for purchase coming from a second mortgage. Typical loan structures under this scenario include 80/10/10 and 80/15/5 transactions. The first reflects a first mortgage equal to eighty percent of the purchase price, a second mortgage equal to ten percent of the home's price, and the borrower putting down ten percent. In the second example, the first mortgage is for eighty percent, the second or Home Equity line or loan covers fifteen percent, and the borrower putting down five percent.

There are a number of benefits for the borrower in opting for piggyback structuring versus a high loan-to-value first mortgage with mortgage insurance:

- The combined monthly payments will usually be lower, or with the same total payment, the borrower will be reducing his or her loan balance by a greater amount;
- Every dollar paid by the borrower goes either for principal or tax deductible interest, whereas there is no such benefit with PMI;
- The borrower has a greater degree of control over the monthly payment. If the Home Equity product used is a line of credit, as the balance on the HELOC is paid down, the required monthly payment decreases. And when the second mortgage is fully repaid, the borrower's monthly principal and interest payment is reduced to just that of the first mortgage amount. If the borrower has PMI and subsequently has it eliminated, he still has the full principal

and interest payment on the original larger first mortgage; and

- Many lenders will pay all or a portion of the closing costs on Home Equity lines and loans. If the lender pays the closing costs for the second mortgage, the borrower saves to the extent that he will be paying the closing costs on a smaller first mortgage.

Here is an example showing the benefits of the piggyback structure when a borrower is putting down less than 20%. Assume the following facts:

1. The home being purchased costs $250,000
2. The borrower is putting down 5%
3. An interest rate of 7.5% on the thirty-year fixed rate first mortgage
4. The second mortgage is also a thirty-year fixed rate loan at 8.5%
5. The mortgage insurance premium for a 95% loan is .75% per year, paid monthly

Option #1	95% first mortgage with private mortgage insurance	
	P& I on the $237,500 first mortgage is	$1,660.63
	The mortgage insurance premium is	148.44
	The total payment is	$1,809.07

Option #2	80% first mortgage and 15% second mortgage	
	P& I on the $200,000 first mortgage is	$1,398.43
	P& I on the $37,500 second mortgage is	288.34
	The total payment is	$1,686.77

In this example, the borrower reduces his monthly payment by $122.30

per month, or $1,467.60 per year using the piggyback loan structure. If this borrower elected to apply the $122.30 monthly savings to his second mortgage payment by making additional principal reduction payments, the second mortgage would be fully paid off in just over twelve years.

Let's use the same example, except that now the second mortgage is in the form of a line of credit, with the required payment being interest only. We'll assume that the interest rate is 6%.

Option #2A 80% first mortgage and 15% second mortgage

P&I on the $200,000 first mortgage is	$1,398.43
Interest on the $37,500 second mortgage is	187.50
The total payment is	$1,585.93

The monthly payment savings is now $223.14 or $2,677.68 per year. Another way to look at this is that the payment is 12% lower than it would have been with the mortgage insurance option. The borrower potentially could have purchased a home that was 12% more expensive and still had the same payment. From the homeowner's perspective, being able to buy "more home" for the same monthly cost is a big benefit. From the loan officer's perspective, he or she benefits to the extent that they are providing a valuable service to their referral sources who benefit from being able to help their customers purchase the best possible home, one that might be a little more expensive than they would otherwise target. A side benefit, but one not to be overlooked, is that if the customer now purchases that more expensive home, the dollar amount of financing originated by the loan officer is greater, increasing that loan officer's commission.

And here is one more way to look at this transaction from a lender's perspective. Assume that there are two lenders competing for the same borrower's business. The first lender can only provide high loan-to-value financing by using mortgage insurance. The second lender offers piggyback financing as an alternative. In order for the first lender to match the overall economics, i.e. monthly payment, loan amortization, and so on, the interest rate on their first mortgage would have to be approximately 6.75%. It is extremely unlikely that the first lender could discount its rate so steeply and still complete the transaction in a profitable manner.

Eliminating the Need for Jumbo Mortgage Financing

This particular use is most applicable for high-end borrowers. It enables these borrowers to structure their transactions to receive potentially the lowest cost and most stable financing package available.

Conventional first mortgage financing transactions can be categorized as either "conforming" or "jumbo". In the case of the former, it means that the loan amount is equal to or less than a certain amount that is established each year by the Federal National Mortgage Corporation (Fannie Mae) and the Federal Home Loan Mortgage Corporation (Freddie Mac). This loan limit establishes the upper end of the size of a loan that these organizations will purchase. [In 2003, the conforming loan limit for single family dwellings was $322,700.] Typically speaking, loans that are of a conforming amount are priced somewhat lower than are jumbo loans. The spread in rates between conforming and jumbo fixed rates of similar term typically ranges from ¼% - ¾%. Or, in order to retain the same pricing as conforming loan amount financing, the borrower may be required to obtain financing other than in the form of a traditional fifteen or thirty-year fixed rate loan. And generally speaking, fixed rate financing is considered more desirable than adjustable rate financing.

Whenever a borrower is either purchasing a home or refinancing a first mortgage and the amount of financing needed exceeds the conforming loan limit, the lender and borrower can examine structuring the transaction using a piggyback second mortgage. The first mortgage loan amount can be up to the conforming loan limit, and the balance of the necessary financing can be in the form of a second mortgage loan or line of credit.

For example, assume that a home buyer is acquiring a home for $500,000 and wishes to put 20% down. Further, we will assume that the conforming loan limit is $322,700. Without the use of a piggyback second mortgage loan or line, the borrower would obtain a $400,000 jumbo mortgage. As an alternative, the transaction could be structured as a $322,700 first mortgage and a $77,300 second mortgage. This enables the borrower to obtain the lowest possible cost fixed rate loan for a significant majority of the necessary financing, with the balance coming in the form of a fixed rate loan or typically adjustable line of credit.

Here is how the payments work out, using the following rates:

Conforming 30-year fixed rate loan	7.5%
Jumbo 30-year fixed rate loan	8.0%
Second mortgage fixed rate with thirty-year amortization 8.5%	

Alternative #1: Jumbo mortgage

$400,000 @ 8%	P&I payment is	$2,935.06

Alternative #2: Conforming first mortgage and piggyback second

$322,700 @ 7.5%	P&I payment is	$2,256.37
$ 77,300 @ 8.5%	P&I payment is	594.37
Total of the two payments		$2,850.74

The monthly savings using the piggyback structure is $84.32 or $1,011.84 per year.

We could take this example a step further. Now assume that the borrower intends to put down 10%, or $50,000 on his $500,000 home purchase. Our two alternatives are to use a $450,000 jumbo loan with mortgage insurance, or a conforming loan amount first mortgage and a $127,300 piggyback second mortgage. Assume the same rates as above, and the mortgage insurance premium on a 90% first mortgage will be set at .48% per year, paid monthly:

Option #1   90% first mortgage with private mortgage insurance

P&I on the $450,000 first mortgage	$3,301.94
The mortgage insurance premium is	180.00
The total payment is	$3,481.94

Option #2   Conforming first and piggyback second

P&I on the $322,700 first mortgage is	$2,256.37
P&I on the $127,300 second mortgage	978.83
The total payment is	$3,235.20

The monthly savings using a structure incorporating a home equity loan is $246.74, or $2,960.92 per year.

Finally, assume that the second mortgage is now in the form of an adjustable rate line of credit at a rate of 6%.

Option #2A Conforming first mortgage and HELOC second mortgage

P&I on the $322,700 first mortgage	$2,256.37
Interest on the $127,300 second mortgage is	636.50
The total payment is	$2,892.87

The monthly reduction in the payment versus the use of a jumbo first mortgage with mortgage insurance is $589.07, or $7,068.84 per year.

Replacement of less advantageous forms of debt

Home Equity financing is often offered by lenders at rates and terms that are considered advantageous when compared with other forms of consumer debt. Credit cards, store charge cards, automobile financing, and other such debts often carry interest rates that are higher than the rates offered by Home Equity lenders. Further, the interest on home equity loans and lines of credit is for many borrowers in many situations tax deductible. When this is the case, that reduces the effective net cost of the financing even further, widening the cost gap between Home Equity financing and other consumer debt.

There will also be times when replacing a mortgage borrower's consumer debt with Home Equity financing will enable the lender to qualify that borrower for a larger first mortgage. An example might be when the borrower has a $10,000 remaining balance on an automobile loan, with a monthly payment of $600. Replace that auto loan with Home Equity financing as part of the structuring of the financing of a home purchase and the net reduction in the borrower's payment from the auto financing could be as much as $500. This $500 savings could increase the home buyer's purchasing power by $50,000 or more. The borrower still needs to be diligent in paying off that $10,000 of financing in a reasonably prompt manner, as the discipline built into the automobile's larger fixed monthly payment will no longer be in place.

Bridge Financing

There are times when home buyers must close on the purchase of a new home before being able to close on the sale of their current residence. The home buyers, however, are counting on the equity in their current home to satisfy all or a portion of the equity requirements for the purchase of the next home. Some lenders provide short-term financing to help handle this situation. This is known as Bridge Financing. The lender funds a home equity loan or line of credit on the current home, and then is repaid upon its sale and closing.

An alternative to this has the lender providing a first mortgage on the new home in the amount that the borrowers planned as their permanent first mortgage. A second mortgage is then funded as well, either a loan or line. When the first home is sold and the equity funds become available, the borrowers pay off or pay down the Home Equity loan on the newly acquired property.

The bridge lender can be at substantial risk, perhaps for a limited reward. To start with, the combined loan-to-value on the property on which the Home Equity loan is being placed is typically going to be very high. At the same time, the borrower is going to have more debt than normal, carrying mortgage payments on both homes until the first residence is sold. The borrower may have a sales contract on the first home, but there is certainly no guarantee that the buyer is going to close on the purchase. And assume that everything works out and that the borrower is able to sell the first home in a fairly prompt manner. The lender only collected interest for a short period of time, perhaps not long enough to justify the time and expense involved in booking the transaction.

Lenders can mitigate some of their risk and make the transaction more financially worthwhile through a number of means. First, it is crucial to make sure that the borrower has the financial reserves and earning power to carry the extra home for a sufficient period of time. Credit, carefully investigating the property value, and all of the other normal underwriting considerations must be handled in an appropriate manner. And then on the income side, lenders will often charge the borrower a fee over and above the interest rate for the bridge loan. They may require the borrower to pay the closing costs, and will otherwise structure the transaction appropriately. And finally, a big inducement for the lender to enter into bridge transactions is the opportunity to provide the financing on the new residence being purchased. The lender may make the terms and/or pricing of the bridge loan more advantageous for the borrower if the financing on the new home is handled by the bridge lender.

Home Improvement and Decorating

If there is equity available, a Home Equity loan is often the most efficient and lowest cost way to finance improvements such as swimming pool additions, upgrading kitchens and baths, roof replacements, major furniture purchases and so on. The home owner should take note that room additions, major home restructuring, and other such projects are perhaps better financed with residential construction and/or home improvement loans. That is something that must be analyzed by the borrower working with the lender to determine the most suitable mortgage product.

Special Events and Education Expenses

Weddings and other celebrations that are usually expensive, as well as college and other education costs are excellent candidates to be paid for with Home Equity financing. It may not be an advantageous time for a homeowner to liquidate investment funds or access other financial resources to pay for these types of expenses. Utilizing the equity on one's home as a ready source of funds for this type of expenditure is often the most cost effective and convenient means for obtaining the needed money.

As a "Just in Case" Reserve

Here, the borrower has no specific or intended use for the loan funds. Typically, a borrower would obtain a HELOC, not drawing down any of the funds and therefore not incurring any interest expense. As many lenders are willing to pay all or a potion of the closing costs, the borrower has very minimal, if any expense exposure if he does not use the line. The borrower can arrange for the availability of funds at a time when he does not need them, and perhaps be able to secure the line of credit under better terms than if the funds were needed on an emergency basis due to a job loss or other financial crisis. This may also be accomplished on a more convenient basis if the line of credit is arranged at the same time as when the borrower is obtaining a first mortgage (either purchase or refinance). The borrower can often submit one application, utilize the same supporting documentation, and attend one combined closing, making the overall process quicker and more convenient.

Home Equity Lending is Important to Lenders and Loan Officers

As indicated at the beginning of this chapter, Home Equity lending is truly a win-win for all of the participants in these transactions.

Profitability

Home Equity lending can be a very profitable area of business for lenders. Many financial institutions value Home Equity loan and line products as an integral portion of their asset holdings, as they offer the potential for high rates of return and protection from interest rate fluctuations. Fixed rate Home Equity loan products are typically priced well above traditional first mortgage rates, often anywhere from one to five percent higher. Interest rates on lines of credit are typically tied to very short-term indices, such as Prime and LIBOR. Lenders are therefore at low risk of holding low yielding fixed rate mortgages in a higher rate environment.

A key component of evaluating the profitability on a portfolio of lines of credit is borrower utilization. Some lenders may charge annual fees or other fees to generate income from these loans, but the primary source of revenue from HELOCS is interest income. And interest income is earned only when borrowers have outstanding balances on their credit lines. Lenders actively involved in Home Equity lending will often have sophisticated campaigns and strategies designed to increase their borrowers' utilization of their credit lines. Mailers and other promotional materials designed to educate and encourage their borrowers may be sent on a regular basis. Some lenders offer their borrowers credit cards tied to their credit lines, so that when the borrower uses the card, the Home Equity facility is drawn upon. Some lenders require draw-downs on their lines at closing, or certain minimum usage of the HELOC, or otherwise the lender may not pay all or a portion of the closing costs or could impose annual fees. All of these strategies, as well as others, are frequently implemented to insure that the lender's portfolio of outstanding HELOCS consists of well-utilized credit lines.

Additional Sales Opportunities

Home Equity lines and loans are an excellent additional sales opportunity for loan originators, helping them build and maintain a growing database of customers. A given client may be a candidate for a new first mortgage perhaps only once every few years. After all, many people stay in their homes five or ten years, or perhaps even longer. First mortgage refinances can be a strong source of business, but typically so when mortgage rates are low. Home Equity mortgages are a way for an astute loan officer to bridge the time period between first mortgage transactions, obtaining business from borrowers who they might not otherwise be able to assist for a number of years. This also enables the loan officer to more closely remain in contact with his or her past borrowers. By remaining in touch with his or her mortgage customers and with them investigating the potential for this additional financing, the loan officer is providing a valuable service and in the process encouraging further repeat and customer-referred business.

More Successful First Mortgage Origination Efforts

Lenders offering a full suite of Home Equity products in conjunction with their first mortgage offerings are able to provide a higher and more complete level of service to their customers. Financial institutions and loan originators who fully utilize Home Equity products as an integral piece of their mortgage sales efforts have a huge advantage over lenders and loan officers not offering Home Equity lending.

Mortgage insurance replacement and the ability to structure around jumbo loans, for example, are two ways in which the utilization of Home Equity financing directly improves the economics of a transaction. Add in the more involved financial planning aspects available and a key ingredient for a long-term lender/customer relationship is created.

Part II

Know This Before Applying

Credit Reports and Credit Scoring
by
Alan Koch

Credit Scores

Credit Bureau Scores were developed in the 1980's to help banks and financial institutions make quick, non-biased decisions and has quickly spread to the mortgage and auto related industries. A Credit Bureau Score is a snapshot of the consumer's credit profile at a certain point in time and summarizes in a number, the risk potential or likelihood that an individual will pay back a loan. The score is based solely on the data within a consumer's credit file and does not use demographic information such as race, color, religion, national origin, gender, age, or marital status.

The most widely used Credit Bureau Scores are "FICO"[SM] or Fair, Isaac scores. FICO scores can range from the 300's to the mid 800's and the higher the score the better credit quality or lower risk. These scores are available from each of the three national credit repositories and each has its own name.

Equifax scores are called BEACON™ scores[*]
Experian scores are called EXPERIAN/FAIR ISAAC scores
Trans Union scores are called EMPERICA™ scores[**]

These scores are calculated by a system of scorecards. These scorecards were developed using thousands of consumers' actual credit reports and applying complex mathematical equations that would evaluate and compare patterns of payments. Weights and measures were assigned to the variables involved and statistical models were created. The types of credit information variables used in these scorecards

51

usually consists of payment history, amounts owed, length of credit history, new credit, and types of credit in use.

Scores are dynamic, meaning they change all the time. Each time a credit report is ordered, the credit profile goes through the scoring process. This allows consumers to be matched with other consumers with similar credit histories. It would not be fair to compare a person with just a few years of credit experience to someone with many years of credit experience. Because of this process, variables can differ from scorecard to scorecard. (Inquiries on one consumer with few years of credit history may not count as much as inquiries on a consumer with many years of established credit.) For a score to be calculated on a credit report, the consumer must have at least one account that has been opened for six months or longer and has had activity within that six month time frame.

Calculations of credit scores are derived from the following factors:

A) Approximately 35% of scores are based on the subject's payment history. A good payment history will certainly help the score. The overall number of derogatory tradelines will also effect the score. Recent delinquencies or items appearing in public records have a major impact on credit scores. If delinquencies or items appearing in the public records are in the distant past, the impact on credit scores will be less than if they are more recently reported.

B) Amounts owed count for approximately 30% of scores. The number of accounts with balances, the balances compared with the available credit limit, and the overall amount owed on all accounts are the factors falling into this category.

C) The length of credit history accounts for approximately 15% of credit scores. How long credit had been established and recent activity on accounts is what is important. The way to avoid damaging credit with respect to credit histories is to avoid opening too many accounts in a short period of time.

D) New credit counts for approximately 10% of credit scores, and types of credit in use count for approximately 10%. How many new accounts and how long since new accounts have been established is key. Re-establishing new credit since having past payment problems will help the score. The number of recent credit related inquiries might have an adverse effect on the score. Shopping for too many accounts may be looked upon as being risky. An inquiry to obtain a copy of a credit report from a credit reporting agency does not count toward the score. All mortgage and auto loan inquiries within a 14-day time frame only count as one inquiry and do not count toward a consumer's score within 30 days from the date a credit report is drawn.

To help lenders understand the score, up to four factor reason codes come with each report. There are approximately 60 possible reason factor codes. Here are a few examples:

    code #10- proportion of balances to credit limits is too high on revolving accounts

    code #14- length of time accounts have been established

    code #22- serious delinquency, derogatory public record, or collection filed

These reason codes shown on the report tell the most important factors in determining the credit score.

In the mortgage industry, it is normal for a lender to order a credit report that merges information from all three repositories and displays all three scores. This allows the lender to see the entire picture of the consumer's credit worthiness. Often the rule for the lender is to use the middle of three scores when three are given, or the lower of two scores if only two bureaus are accessed.

Fair Isaac states that, based on the FICO scores of the general population of the United States, 20% score below 620, 20% between

620 and 690, 20% between 690 and 740, 20% between 740 and 780, and 20% over 780.

Credit Reports

A credit report details financial obligations an individual has with banks, retailers, credit unions, mortgage companies, and financial institutions. Typically found in a credit report is information regarding the creditor, account numbers, open dates of the accounts, types of accounts, terms, amount of credit or loan, payment amounts, balances and any amounts past due. These accounts, including accounts that have been closed or paid off, usually remain on a credit record for seven years. A revolving credit arrangement can remain on the record for an infinite period of time as long as it is being used. This information is supplied to the three national repositories, Equifax, Experian, and Trans Union on a monthly basis via magnetic tape. The tapes report on open, paid, current and past due accounts that creditors have in their database. The three repositories sell the credit reports to other credit grantors so they can check payment histories and credit scores and decide whether or not to grant credit.

Public Records information including bankruptcies, tax liens, and judgments is also included in the report and is usually supplied directly from the Public Records of local Court Houses. Public Records information usually remains on credit records for a period of seven years with the exception of bankruptcies, which remain on the record for a period of ten years, and open tax liens, which can remain for fifteen years.

Credit reports show in detail inquiries that have been made in the last two years. These inquiries usually display the lender or credit grantor, the date, and in some cases, the type of credit requested.

Information about a consumer's credit profile can differ from repository to repository. For instance, a local bank, retailer or credit

54

union may elect to report to only one repository to save on the costs associated with reporting to all three. The same account may be reported differently to each of the three repositories because of delays in getting the automated tape to a specific repository in time. (Example: one repository shows the account as current, the second shows the account as current but with the notation that it was thirty days past due at one time, and the third shows that the account is currently thirty days delinquent.) Even though it is the same account, it could be reported three different ways.

Family members with the same name sometimes have their files mixed with other family members with the same name. They may both live at the same residence, but even with different social security numbers and birth dates it is still possible for the bureaus to mix up the accounts. Sometimes human errors can happen and data is input incorrectly. A payment could be posted incorrectly or be applied to an incorrect account number.

For these reasons, it is recommended that every consumer get a copy of his or her credit report at least once a year from each repository. All three repositories have web sites where reports can be requested for a nominal fee, usually $8. An exception to this is made for a person who is denied credit, in which case a copy of the credit report should be provided for free. These reports can be ordered directly from the repositories through a simple Internet search.

Consumers have the right to challenge any inaccuracies reported. The procedure for this is to notify the repository of the dispute on the accounts to be challenged. The repository will send out a dispute form on behalf of the client to the creditor(s) named. The creditor(s) then has thirty days (twenty business days) to respond to the dispute. Should a response not be returned within this time period, the subject has the right to request that the item be changed to the status requested. If a response comes back, but the consumer still disagrees with the result, they have the right to enter a consumer statement of up to 100 words on the credit report explaining the dispute.

In the middle of the twentieth century, using credit was a sign of weakness. People were taught to save and pay cash for everything. Asking for credit, except perhaps in the instances of purchasing a home or automobile, meant that a person did not save enough cash to pay for purchases. Times have changed! Now, credit is used for every purpose imaginable.

Establishing credit can be as easy as going to a bank and sitting down with the manager to discuss credit needs. Most banks can issue their own credit cards and will be willing to extend limited lines until credit is established. It can begin small with a limit of $300, and then grow to $500. It is often best to meet face to face with a manager or credit officer as opposed to simply making an application for credit. This may help expedite the approval process and give the applicant an opportunity to explain any potential credit issues and have his intent be better understood.

From the initial time credit is established the best way to proceed to building credit is to borrow or charge a small amount and pay it back immediately. Then repeat this process perhaps even increasing the amount of the borrowings. The important thing to remember is to continually pay all amounts owed when they become due, to never miss a due date, and preferably pay off all amounts when due as opposed to making minimum allowable payments. Once credit has been established, the idea is to maintain it, and the only way to maintain credit is to repay it according to the terms outlined in the credit agreement.

*BEACON is a registered trademark of Equifax
**EMPERICA is a registered trademark of Trans Union
FICO is a service mark of Fair Isaac and company

Adjustable Rate Mortgages
by
Patrick Mansell

Since the early 1930's and for the next fifty years, the thirty year fixed rate mortgage was the standard in residential real estate finance. During that entire time interest rates tended to be stable and moved in a narrow range year after year. In the late 1970's and early 1980's the country's economy experienced a period of rapid inflation. In an effort to avoid some very serious consequences, like a depression or a complete collapse of our economy, the Federal Reserve began raising interest rates to slow things down. The short-term prime rate, which is the interest rate banks charge to their most creditworthy borrowers, rose to over twenty percent at some banks. Long term interest rates for home loans rose to above 18%. That slowed things down very fast. Fewer people were willing to or could afford to buy homes, and businesses cut their borrowing down to the barest necessity. The housing industry, which is heavily reliant on the supply and cost of money, was thrown into a tailspin. Many homebuilders were forced out of business during this critical period of inflation and high interest rates.

To help home buyers afford housing and qualify for mortgage loans adjustable rate mortgages (ARMs) became popular. These loans usually start with lower interest rates to make payments more manageable in their early years. ARMs are also favored by lenders because it allows them to match their fluctuating cost of funds to the income from the mortgage money they lend.

How do they work?

With most ARMs the interest rate changes every year, every three years or every five years. However, some ARMs have more frequent interest and payment changes. The period between one rate change and the next is called the adjustment period. A loan with an adjustment period of one year is called a one year ARM and the interest rate can change once every year. Many of the three and five year ARMs actually convert to one year ARMs after the initial three or five year terms, and these are referred to as three-one ARMs and five-one ARMs.

The periodic adjustments for ARMs are made based upon the movement of what is known as an index. As that index changes so will the interest rate on mortgages that are tied to that index. Popular indices include the one year Treasury index (CMT which stands for Constant Maturity Treasury), the COFI index (Eleventh District Cost of Funds Index) a measure of the cost of money to the district banks under the San Francisco Federal Reserve. LIBOR, (London Interbank Offered Rate) is becoming more and more popular as it is a well recognized index internationally, which in turn makes banks from all over the world more comfortable with the securities backed by mortgages using this index, helping to create a more liquid market for this type of ARM.

To determine the interest rate on an ARM lenders add to the index a few percentage points called the 'margin'. While the amount of the margin will differ from lender to lender and from loan to loan, whatever it is fixed at when the loan is made will usually remain constant throughout the life of the loan. As an example, when adjustment time rolls around and the index is pegged at 2.25% and the margin is 2.50%, that loan will adjust to 4.75% (the sum of the 2.25% index value and the 2.50% margin) for the next adjustment period. In comparing ARM programs between different lenders a borrower would need to familiarize himself with the index and margin that lender uses. Two lenders might each use the CMT index for adjustments to the interest rate, but one may charge a 2.5% margin while the other charges 4%. In the example above of an index value of 2.25%, at adjustment time one loan would adjust to 4.75% while the other would adjust to 6.25%. This concept is simply explained and understood, and is the basis for a borrower protecting himself from entering into a very expensive ARM agreement.

Not only should a consumer be familiar with the margin that a lender will charge, but some familiarity with the index used and the history of that index will also be useful. Generally the history of the CMT index has shown it to be relatively unstable in the respect that its swings are somewhat more extreme than the movements of the COFI index. On the other hand, the COFI index moves in a narrower range and tends to be lower than the CMT. Histories of these indices can be found by a simple Internet search. With that information in hand a borrower can do his own analysis of the ARMs different lenders are offering to see which loan offer suits him best.

Interest Rate and Payment Caps

No discussion of ARMs would be complete without mentioning the subject of caps. Caps are limits on the amount of adjustments that can be made to payments or to interest rates during the life of the loan.

There are several types of caps that can be applied to adjustable rate mortgages that provide safety and affordability to the borrower. Under the subject of safety for the borrower is the topic of interest rate caps. There are two ways in which interest rates can be capped in adjustable rate financing: periodic interest rate caps and life of loan caps. The menu of combinations of this kind of caps is endless. Periodic rate caps are limits placed on any single adjustment to the rate. Typically ARMs are written in such a way that the interest rate on the loan can adjust by no more than a certain percentage upward or downward on any single adjustment. A loan with a 2% annual cap that today carries a rate of 5.25% can adjust to no more than 7.25% or less than 3.25% at its next adjustment. A typical life of loan cap, meaning a cap that limits the upside adjustments for the entire life of the loan, might be set at 6% over the initial interest rate of the loan. An ARM with a start rate of 5.0% and a 6% life of loan cap cannot exceed 11% during its entire life.

Most often ARMs are written with annual and life caps. A typical ARM may be expressed as a Treasury ARM having a start rate (initial rate) of 5.0% with a 2.75% margin and 2/6 caps. This is translated as a one year adjustable rate mortgage starting at 5.0% with future adjustments pegged to the CMT index plus 2.75%, and on which the rate cannot exceed 7.0% or be less than 3.0% on the first adjustment, and that will never exceed 11.0% over its entire life. The rate caps set the boundaries by which future adjustments will be limited. Another example of the same thing might be a loan expressed as a one year COFI (Cost Of Funds Index) ARM loan at 5.0% with a 2.40% margin and 1/5 caps. Translated this means the loan is a one year adjustable rate mortgage with annual adjustments based upon the movement of the Cost Of Funds Index plus a margin of 2.40%, and on which the rate at the first adjustment will not be greater than 6.0% or less than 4.0%, and that can never exceed 10.0%. These rate caps are built in safety features that protect the borrower against sudden spikes in interest rates and excessive adjustments over the life of the loan.

Payment caps add to the overall affordability of adjustable rate financing but do not provide the safety net that interest rate caps do. A payment cap is simply a limit upon how much a borrower will have to pay on its next adjustment regardless of how much the interest rate has changed. For example suppose a LIBOR indexed loan is written with annual payment caps of 7.5% and no annual interest rate caps. In this example the payment cap of 7.5% means that regardless of how much the interest rate rises between adjustments, the borrower can elect to cap his principal and interest payment increase to 7.5% of the payment he was paying during the previous adjustment period. As an example, assume a mortgage loan of $250,000 and an interest rate of 5% which has a monthly payment of $1,342, and that adjusts to 7% in the second year. The initial year's monthly principal and interest payment is $1,342 (rounded). The fully amortizing payment at the fully indexed rate after the adjustment is $1,663 (also rounded), a 23% increase over year one.

Now suppose the borrower elects the payment cap of 7.5% above the previous year's payment. His new payment rate will be $1,442. While this periodic payment cap might help the borrower to afford his payments at a time when interest rates are climbing, it can also end up with a bad result. The borrower pays $1,442 in the face of a $1,663 accrual rate. This means that the election was made to defer the payment of $321 per month by electing payment caps. That $321 does not simply go away. It is called 'deferred interest' and is added to the outstanding balance of the loan. At the end of the year the loan balance would actually be increased by the amount of deferred interest, in this case $3,852. This deferred interest is termed 'negative amortization' which serves to make the payments affordable, but also has the effect of increasing the borrower's debt. There is a great deal of controversy about the benefits of negative amortization and it should be thoroughly understood before being implemented.

The subject of caps can begin to become quite complicated. For example an adjustable rate mortgage can have interest rate and payment caps. In fact, most of the payment capped ARMs do have rate caps as well. As an example, suppose an ARM loan is expressed as a COFI ARM with a 2.40% margin, 2/5 interest rate caps with payment caps of 7.5% per year. On this loan not only is the interest rate adjusting annually within the 2% annual and 5% lifetime limits, but the borrower also has the right to cap his payments should the index move against him in so unfavorable a way as to require a payment increase of more than the 7.5% cap. Should the borrower elect to pay based upon the payment cap, he would be experiencing negative amortization within a rate capped environment. The way in which negative amortization is recovered by the lender is through re-amortization of the loan at each adjustment. In the event that the borrower in the example above elected to defer $1,500 of interest and add that to the balance of his loan, at the next adjustment the lender would calculate his new payment using the factor for that year's interest rate and remaining term, times the new outstanding balance, which in this example is $1,500 higher than it was the previous year. All one-year adjustable rate mortgages are re-amortized each year, but the difference in this example is that the new payment will be based upon the higher loan balance as opposed to an ARM without payment caps, which will be subject to normal amortization.

Initial Terms and Adjustments

A popular vehicle in adjustable rate financing is the loan with a longer initial term and annual adjustments thereafter. Three, five, seven and ten year initial terms are often used in the place of fixed rate mortgages when the situation warrants. Because fixed rate financing is often more expensive, borrowers who know that for one reason or another they might not be in a home for more than a specified period of time, might opt for the ARM with the longer initial term.

A three-one ARM is a mortgage that is fixed for the first three years and then adjusts to a one year adjustable after the initial period. Five-one, seven-one and ten-one ARMs operate similarly except that the initial term is longer. There are several issues of relevance when considering one of these ARMs with the longer initial term, two of which are of critical importance and knowledge of which can mean a great deal of difference in whether the loan suits the borrower as much as it might appear.

Sometimes in ARMs with longer initial terms, the caps might be described exactly as they would be on a one year adjustable, such as a five-one ARM at 5.50% with a 2.75% margin and 2/6 caps. Because the loan is expressed this way does not necessarily mean that the first adjustment will be capped at 7.50%. It is not uncommon for the actual wording of the adjustable rate rider, that document that attaches to the note and expresses the terms for future adjustments, to read that the 2% annual cap kicks in after the first adjustment. What this means is that the index for this loan has been changing for the past five years, and on the fifth anniversary date of the loan the rate for the first adjustment is now in effect. Five years is enough time to go through a complete interest rate cycle and that index value that might have been 2.75% when the loan was cast, could have climbed to 5.75% in the intervening five years. Now the new rate based upon the formula of index plus margin will be 8.50%. The 2% annual cap did not apply to this first adjustment.

Another potential area of concern has to do with the floor rate for some adjustable rate mortgages. As in the example above, suppose a five-one loan starts at 5.50% and the ARM rider expresses that the loan shall also carry a floor rate, the minimum rate allowable for the loan, of the initial rate. This means the rate can never adjust below 5.50% for its entire life. If when the adjustment comes around at the end of the fifth year, and the index has fallen to 1%, the borrower in this instance would be committed to paying at least the floor rate even though the formula for adjustments would have given him a rate of 2.75% (the margin) plus 1% (the index) or 3.75%.

Convertible ARMs -Having it Both Ways

Convertible Adjustable Rate Mortgages give the borrower the option at certain times in the future to switch over to a fixed rate mortgage. The convertible feature is usually provided as an addendum to the note and sets forth the terms under which the conversion can take place. Conversions have limitations of which the borrower should be aware. A typical example would be that the conversion can only take place on an anniversary date within the first five years. Another might be that the loan can only be converted on the first, second or third anniversary. Other conversions are more liberal and may provide that the conversion can take place at any time during the life of the loan.

It would be an oversimplification to say that a convertible ARM will convert to the current market for fixed rate mortgages at the time of conversion. That would leave open to interpretation exactly what is meant by 'market rate'. While it is true that the rate at conversion will be tied to the then prevailing rate when the loan converts, the exact formula for a conversion should be much more precise. This conversion feature will be tied to an index just as all other adjustments under the ARM will be. Typically a conversion option will be written in such a way that there is no mistaking how the loan will adjust. Commonly lenders will use the Fannie Mae sixty day price for thirty year fixed rate mortgages plus 5/8%. Other formulae can be used as well, and it is a good practice for the borrower to be familiar with this formula so he/she can know what to expect upon conversion.

The Impact of Adjustable Rate Mortgages

Federal Home Loan Mortgage Corporation (Freddie Mac) claims that adjustable rate mortgages account for 20% of the mortgages in the United States. This would appear to be a low figure when one takes into account that there are only two types of mortgages, fixed rate and adjustable. As important an impact as this has had on the affordability of home mortgages, it is equally important to the overall mortgage market in general. With adjustable rate financing a new avenue of investment was opened to commercial banks and other traditional depository institutions. It has bred competition among lenders and provided liquidity to the mortgage market, which in turn has made the dream of home ownership a reality for millions of American families.

Loan Amortization
by
Patrick Mansell

It is a daunting prospect for a borrower to think about going to a closing table and setting up a new loan, whether it be to refinance old debt or purchase a new home, and to know he will have to live with that monthly payment for the next thirty years. While mortgage financing is a necessary part of most real estate transactions, it does not necessarily mean that facing 360 mortgage payments, spanning a generation in time, is a pleasant thing. In fact, shortening that payment schedule can not only give peace of mind, but understanding loan amortization can be one of the biggest money savers in the area of mortgage finance.

The root of the word 'amortization' is derived from the Latin word 'mort' which means die or death. To amortize a loan is to give it a slow death. And to make a loan amortize requires that every monthly payment contains a partial principal payment that allows the loan to pay off a little bit at a time. Some loans, like interest only loans never die, they just go on and on. But that is rarely the case in residential mortgage finance. Nearly all of these types of loan amortize.

The easiest way to understand where the big money savings comes from is to have knowledge of what it is that comprises the monthly payment. The answer is that it is: part interest and part principal. The amount of interest paid comes from a calculation based upon a simple formula. In the mathematical question, "How is monthly interest calculated?" The answer is derived from the equation that states the following: the monthly interest payment is equal to the outstanding principal balance of the loan, times the interest rate, divided by twelve. Here is a simple example: where the initial loan amount is $50,000, the annual interest rate is 8%. Here is how the equation works: the 8% interest on $50,000 equals $4,000 (that is for a whole year); just divide the $4,000 by 12. Thus, $4,000 divided by 12 equals $333.33. That is the monthly interest for a loan that begins the month with a $50,000 balance and carries an annual interest rate of 8%.

In this example, if only the $333.33 was applied to the payment, only the interest would have been paid. But because a borrower and a lender both have the goal of having the loan eventually pay off, a portion of the principal of the loan has to be paid as well. Factor tables tell how much principal needs to be included in each payment to make the loan amortize. The tables are set up to help determine how much should paid monthly to make the loan amortize over any given number of years. Just as an example, to make the loan above amortize in thirty years, a factor based upon an interest rate of 8% and a thirty year term is used. The factor for that combination is .0073376. The factor, times the loan amount, gives the monthly payment to fully amortize the loan. Using that factor the calculation for the monthly payment works out to be $366.88. Recall that in the first month of the loan, the interest is still $333.33 because the loan balance in the beginning of the month was $50,000. The additional $33.55 went to pay down principal on the loan. And this is where amortization begins. In the second month the same payment is made, $366.88, but a different result is achieved. A little less interest is paid and a little more of the payment goes to principal. That is because the principal balance in the beginning of the second month was no longer $50,000. Remember, the first payment included $33.55 in principal, so the beginning balance in the second month is $49,966.45. That changes everything. Not by very much, but by enough to make a difference over thirty years. As it works out, the interest portion of the second month's payment is $333.11 and the principal reduction is $33.77. It's only 22 cents different from the previous month. Not much, but it will soon begin to add up.

In the third month the beginning balance is now $67.32 less than the original balance and the interest for the month will be calculated on $49,932.68 instead of $50,000. The lesson here is that month after month a little more principal is paid down, meaning that less of the payment goes to interest and more is applied to principal. This has a snowball effect so that in the later years of the loan, when a good portion of principal has been paid, the amortization intensifies to the point that the interest portion becomes insignificant and the principal portion becomes very noticeable.

Factor tables give the calculation for loans of any length (term), twenty years, ten, fifteen, even thirteen years and four months if that is how long the borrower wants. In modern real estate finance in America the thirty year loan is relatively standard. It was promoted this way in the early twentieth century as a way to make homes more affordable for the average family. A loan paying off over that term has a very low payment because there is so little principal paid in the early years.

Any prepayment of principal will serve to shorten the term of the loan and will save on interest expense. The reason for this goes back to the original formula for the calculation of monthly interest: principal outstanding, times the interest rate, divided by twelve. In the example above where the loan was chugging along at a thirty year rate, only a little over $33 was going toward principal in the early months. Now suppose the borrower applies a payment of $10,000 to reduce the balance of the loan. Interest is no longer accruing on $50,000; it is now based on $40,000. In the formula: interest rate, times principal balance, divided by twelve, if the payment remains the same and the interest rate remains the same, and the money is still outstanding for one month, something has to give. There is only one other variable that can change, and that is the term. This means that with the other parts of the equation being constant, that $10,000 prepayment of principal will create a new amortization schedule that will necessarily shorten the term. In this example where the loan balance has been reduced to $40,000 and the interest rate is 8% and the payment is $366.88, a new amortization schedule will show that the loan will now pay off in 16.23 years.

This example is important for several reasons. It points out that prepaid principal payments shorten the term of the loan in a dramatic way. Any principal reduction, whether it is adding an extra hundred dollars per month to the scheduled payment to pay the loan off sooner, or taking a shorter term loan to start off with, the result will be a great deal of interest savings.

A popular alternative to the thirty year mortgage is the a loan that is scheduled with a fifteen year amortization. While the payment on a fifteen year mortgage is somewhat higher than the payment on a thirty year amortizing loan, the interest savings for this loan is impressive. The below Illustration 1 shows the amortization of each of these loans in the first five months.

Illustration 1

	30 year loan			15 year loan		
	$366.88			$477.82		
Payment						
Month	Interest	Principal	Balance	Interest	Principal	Balance
1	333.33	33.55	49,966.45	333.33	144.49	49,855.51
2	333.11	33.77	49,932.68	332.37	145.45	49,710.05
3	332.88	34.00	49,898.68	331.40	146.42	49,563.63
4	332.66	34.22	49,864.46	330.42	147.40	49,416.23
5	332.43	34.45	49,830.01	329.44	148.30	49,267.85

What happened here was that in the first month of each of these loans the amount of interest paid was the same. Each had an outstanding balance of $50,000 for thirty days and an interest rate of 8%. Each of the loans paid interest in the amount of $333.33 as was demonstrated earlier. The formula did not change. What changed was the payment. To amortize the loan over fifteen years required a payment of $477.82. The difference between the total payment and the interest portion of the payment equals the amount of principal that was applied. Quite simply, $477.82 payment, minus $333.33 in interest, equals a principal reduction of $144.49, and a loan balance after the first payment of $49,855.51. On the thirty year loan a payment of only $366.88 was made but the same $333.33 was necessary to pay the interest, so only $33.55 in principal was paid. The loan balance after the first payment on the thirty year loan was $49,966.45. Each subsequent month's interest is calculated on the then outstanding balance, and the amount of interest required to service the loan is reduced. Since the payment remains the same, more of the payment goes to principal and less to interest. The result of this compounding is demonstrated by noting the effect of the additional principal applications after the first five months. The loan balance on the thirty year loan after five payments is $49,830.01 whereas the balance on the fifteen year loan after five payments is $49,267.85. The difference after only five payments is $562.15. This amount is greater than if you take the difference in the payments and multiply that by five. That would be only $111.06 times five or $555.30. Why is there a $6.85 difference? The answer is in the amount of accumulated interest on each loan. This is tied to the fact that the interest required to service the debt on the fifteen year loan becomes less and less each month because of the rapid amortization of the principal balance.

The dynamics at work here are interesting. The principal balance is coming down very rapidly on the fifteen year loan for several reasons. First of all, the entire amount of the difference in the payments between the two terms ($366.88 vs. $477.82 or $111.06) is applied to principal. And secondly, because the balance on the fifteen year loan starts off lower in the second month, the interest portion of the payment is less than with the thirty year loan. Notice that in the first month the interest is the same for each loan. But this is true for only one month. This repeats and compounds itself in each subsequent month until the loan is finally paid off.

Illustration 1 shows the effect of rapid amortization in the first five months of the loan. The real drama is in the effect this compounding has over the life of the two loans. While the fifteen year loan payment is only $110.96 more than the payment on the thirty year loan, the interest savings is remarkable as Illustration 2 demonstrates.

Illustration 2

Loan Amount	$50,000.00	$50,000.00
Term	30 years	15 years
Interest Rate	8%	8%
Monthly Payment	$ 366.88	$ 477.82
Number of Payments	360	180
Total of Payments	$132,076.80	$86,007.60
Total Interest Paid	$ 82,076.80	$36,007.60

Notice from this illustration that the sum of the 360 payments made on the thirty year loan equals $132,076.80 while the sum of the payments on the fifteen year loan is 180 payments totaling $86,007.60. The calculation for the sum of the interest payments is simply the total payments less the original principal balance of the loan ($50,000 in this example). On the thirty year loan a total of $82,076.80 in interest was scheduled over the life of the loan. On the fifteen year loan interest of only $36,007.60 was scheduled. More than twice as much interest was scheduled on the thirty year loan as opposed to the fifteen year loan and the difference in payments was only $110.92 per month.

In addition to the interest savings generated through the rapid amortization of a shorter term mortgage schedule, there is an added bonus that most lenders will offer. Generally a shorter term mortgage will require a somewhat lower interest rate than the loan with the full thirty year term. In real terms the greatest tradeoff between savings for a shorter term and scheduling a payment that is actually affordable is in matching the thirty year mortgage to the fifteen year mortgage. There are also breaks for twenty year loans and ten year loans but the difference is not so great. In the instance of the twenty year loan, the interest break can be from very little to almost negligible. The ten year scheduled amortization will carry a lower rate than the fifteen year loan but this begins to get into an area where the payments required to support a ten year amortization schedule become much less affordable.

In rough terms a fifteen year mortgage may require an interest rate approximately one half percentage point below the rate required for a thirty year loan. In the above example of a thirty year loan in the amount of $50,000 at and interest rate of 8%, the fifteen year loan might require a rate of only 7.5%. In this way, not only is the total interest paid reduced on account of the more rapid amortization of the principal, but it is further offset by being set at a lower rate from the beginning. Illustration 3 points this out.

Illustration 3

	30 year loan	15 year loan
Interest Rate	8%	7.50%
Payment (P&I)	$ 366.88	$ 463.50
Total Payments	$132,076.80	$83,430.00
Total Interest	$ 82,076.80	$33,430.00

Again the fifteen year loan outshines the thirty year term. The life of loan interest savings is now $48,646.80 while the monthly payment is only $96.62 more than the longer term loan. This is another argument for the shorter term mortgage schedule and an excellent illustration of why knowledge of loan amortization can be an important source of money savings.

The Role of the Commercial Bank in Mortgage Lending
by
Thom Bambenek

When thinking of where to go to get a residential loan, most people would probably not think of going to their local commercial bank. Instead, they would ask their realtor, a neighbor, a local savings & loan (that now calls itself a bank), or a mortgage broker. The interesting thing is that a commercial bank may be the actual provider of the funds used to make the residential loan from many of the previously mentioned sources of residential financing.

While realtors do not usually provide mortgage financing directly, they are a great referral source to lenders who do provide the financing. In many cases, it is the realtor's commercial bank where they maintain their checking and escrow accounts that can also provide the required first and/or second mortgage to acquire a property. When necessary, a commercial bank can also provide the financing to acquire a building lot where someone eventually wants to construct a home. Once the lot is acquired, the commercial bank can provide a construction/permanent mortgage loan. This type of loan can pay off the lot loan used to acquire the land, and provide the property owner the construction funds to build his dream home. The construction period can be anywhere from six months to two years or more depending on the size of the home to be built and the complexity of the building project.

During the construction phase of the loan, the title is checked to make sure the commercial bank remains in the first lien position and that no liens are filed by any of the contractors or subcontractors working on the home. While this protects the bank it should also reassure the borrower that their investment is being protected. In addition to checking title to the property, periodic inspections of the

73

construction are also done to make sure the home is being built following the architect's plans and specifications.

While the construction/permanent loan is usually made to the individuals who are having their home built, a commercial bank can also offer builders either lines of credit or individual construction/permanent loans in the builder's name. In this instance the builder retains ownership of the property until construction is complete, at which time a buyer takes possession of the completed property. In this type of financing the buyer of the home would qualify for and assume the builder's loan which would simultaneously convert to a permanent mortgage.

Thus, commercial banks play a much greater role in community lending than simply offering checking or savings accounts. In fact commercial banks play an active role in providing residential mortgage financing to all segments of the local community from low income to the ultra wealthy.

For the low-to-moderate income families, commercial banks provide special lending programs that offer long term financing to assist in trying to make housing affordable for as many qualified individuals as possible. This is being done so that commercial banks adequately address the Community Reinvestment Act (CRA) which requires banks to help fulfill the credit needs of all borrowers in their market areas. To help accomplish this, commercial banks on their own or as a part of organized groups, such as CDC (Community Development Corporation), housing authorities, and governmental agencies, reach out to find individuals of low-to-moderate income who want to be homeowners. Once these individuals are identified, they are put through a mortgage application process to determine if they qualify for a mortgage. If they do not qualify, the reasons for denial of a mortgage request can be addressed and corrected so the person can ultimately be approved. Many times credit problems show up on an applicant's credit report which may or may not be valid. Applicants are assisted in credit counseling to address and resolve as many credit issues as possible so that they can move forward in the mortgage approval process.

Home buyer educational classes are held to help educate the applicants on the true responsibilities of homeownership. Issues like budgeting, closing costs, title insurance and home repairs are all addressed so as few surprises as possible confront these homebuyers. An integral part of this process the is offering of long term fixed rate financing with as little as 3% to 5% down payment. On top of this, mortgage insurance, a very expensive part of home financing which would typically be required, is often waived by many lenders involved in these programs. This is an advantage offered by commercial banks that can rarely be matched by mortgage brokers and mortgage bankers.

Aid in the form of forgivable loans and grants are also often available to assist the low-to-moderate income borrowers acquire their properties. These loans and grants are usually forgivable after the borrower lives in the property for a specified period of time, usually at least 5 years. In many cases there is no interest charged as long as the borrowers live in the property.

While commercial banks provide many services to individuals or groups related to residential financing, they are also actively involved in residential financing themselves and have employees whose full time job is to seek out individuals to whom they can extend residential loans. Because of this a neighbor or friend may have received their mortgage directly from a commercial banker. Most commercial banks, while offering loan products that may be meant for their own portfolio, can also offer all the mortgage products available in the industry. Advances in technology and the way mortgage loans are made and sold make these programs very accessible. Again, while many people might not think of going to a commercial bank for a residential loan, a commercial bank is able to meet most mortgage needs and, in many cases, is the provider of the funds to make the loans.

Besides residential first and second mortgages, commercial banks also offer commercial real estate loan products to builder/developers. They help finance the acquisition and development of raw land, along with the lines of credit required to build anything from a single home to entire subdivisions. They can finance condos and town home projects in addition to many types of commercial properties including apartments, office buildings and shopping centers.

Commercial banks also provide lending services and products to many individuals and groups involved in the residential lending process, such as mortgage brokers, mortgage lenders, and many governmental and not-for-profit organizations involved in the lending of money to individuals to purchase their homes. Commercial banks lend to mortgage brokers so they have the money to fund mortgage closings. Warehousing lines of credit are provided to mortgage lenders to assure they have funds to close loans and meet their commitments.

Governmental agencies may use commercial banks to hold and invest funds, to help issue bonds, to maintain the accounts for cities and governmental bodies, such as tax collectors. Many times there is a competitive bidding process to be awarded the depository relationship with cities, counties and government agencies. As part of this process, the successful bidder is usually one who provides all the required financial products at competitive prices. But also an institution that can clearly show its commitment to the community it serves and the organization whose accounts it wants. In other words, they must prove they are a good corporate citizen in action and deeds and not just words a commercial bank's CRA record. In lending to the community education is an integral part of this process and it is fair to say the institution awarded an account relationship would also have demonstrated a very strong CRA commitment.

Not-for-profit groups look to commercial banks to make available creative and affordable financing alternatives to the clients they serve to help them to become homeowners. They also look to commercial banks to provide financial assistance to them so they can accomplish their stated goals. This can be done through grants, in-kind donations, support of fund raising activities and other charitable events and functions.

Commercial banks are an integral part of the entire financial structure and in particular make huge commitments to the communities they serve from many different access points. Persons desiring professional financial assistance, whether it be for mortgage financing or other borrowing needs, are well served by contacting their commercial bank to see what it might be able to offer and how it fits into their own particular circumstance.

Since the mid 1980's the role of the commercial bank in residential lending, on a national basis, has grown tremendously. This growth was also spurred by the consolidation and mergers of commercial banks that have taken place over the last two decades.

Commercial banks initially, and still today, made fixed rate residential mortgages for sale, as they did not want to experience the problems of their savings and loan counterparts that kept fixed rate loans in their portfolios only to see the interest rate environment move against them and ultimately lead to the collapse of the industry as they knew it. Twenty years ago commercial banks, while making and selling fixed rate mortgages, were also developing and pioneering the adjustable rate mortgage (ARM) with adjustment terms of 1, 3, 5, 7 and even 10 years and amortization as long as 30 years. These ARMs were usually tied to a well defined index, U. S. Treasury or others, with a margin for profit built in above the base index. This gave the loans the ability to move up or down with the market index used and presented much less risk over time than fixed rate mortgages.

77

The advent of ARM products, along with increased technology and a sophisticated financial market, made it increasingly easy to make and sell mortgage loans at a profit in all types of markets.

Commercial banks seizing and recognizing these advantages also realized that if they could make a residential loan to a customer on whom they had a very complete financial picture, they also had a much higher likelihood of cross selling multiple products to the same customer. This cross selling ability was and still is at the heart of why commercial banks have aggressively embraced residential mortgage lending, so much so that Wells Fargo, through its mortgage affiliate and branch operations, has become the largest residential lender in America. In fact, of the top twenty residential lenders in America in 2002, ten where commercial banks.

Part III

Mortgage Handling

The Loan Application Process
by
Robert Lurer

A key component to the success of closing a mortgage loan begins at the first contact with the loan officer or lending institution. The first impression of both the applicant and loan officer is often a lasting one and many relationships either succeed or fail because of first impressions. Preparation for the initial call by both the applicant and loan officer is an important element when applying for a loan. Often a referral from a friend, neighbor or other source has given the applicant the benefit of their experience in dealing with a specific loan originator.

During the initial telephone interview, it is helpful if the loan officer can qualify the applicant and identify any applicant constraints. Many successful loan originators like to gauge discussing applicant constraints based upon how the telephone conversation is going, fearing they may loose the opportunity to set a firm appointment if an applicant is "scared off" by questions that may seem too intrusive. On the other hand, it may be a waste of time to set an appointment with a loan officer if there is no chance of having him supply the desired financing.

When a firm date and time for the meeting is set up, the applicant should ask the loan officer what information and documents he should bring to the face-to-face interview. In most cases, the applicant should be prepared to present a recent paycheck stub, recent bank and investment statements and, depending upon the policy of the lending company contacted, an application fee. The applicant should always ask how the fee will be applied. If the fee is non-refundable and is not applicable to any out-of-pocket costs, it may be a signal to the applicant to look elsewhere. It is not uncommon, however, to be asked to pay an up-front fee to be used to cover the cost of an appraisal and credit report.

The things to remember about the initial meeting are:
- The applicant and loan officer should strive to be on time.
- Make sure that both the applicant and loan officer are prepared.
- Make sure the loan officer is professional.
- Be confident and at ease.
- Make sure the loan officer identifies the applicant's constraints.
- Make sure the loan officer qualifies the applicant before exiting the face-to-face interview.
- Choose a loan officer that acts as an adviser, not just an application taker.

The first item listed above may be more important than it appears. Because a relationship must be developed between the loan officer and the applicant, his first commitment to you, that of being on time, may be an indicator of future performance.

Being prepared is also important as time may be critical. In purchase transactions, the clock is ticking from the minute the applicant signs the purchase contract. Delays in processing time caused by a partial delivery of required documents that the loan officer has requested could lead to increased pressure and tension on everyone connected to the transaction. When considering entering into a financing transaction, whether for the purchase of real estate or the refinancing of an existing loan, it is best for the applicant to spend a fair amount of time thinking through concerns, predispositions, preferred financing terms and any perceived obstacles that may have to be overcome. The applicant should list those specific goals the he wishes to achieve, beyond just getting the loan at a great rate.

The applicant and loan officer should explore the following questions:
- What is the best type of loan for the borrower?
- Should the loan have a fixed rate or adjustable rate?
- How about an adjustable interest rate loan possessing an extended fixed interest rate period before the interest rate begins to adjust?
- How long does the borrower intend to own the property?
- What is the greatest priority, a lower payment or quicker build up of equity?
- Does it suit the applicant better to make a larger down payment or to pay the additional cost associated with a smaller down payment?
- Would a combination first and second mortgage be suitable?

A loan officer not prepared to discuss the loan, interest rates, loan terms and alternative loan plans may be another gauge of things to come. An experienced loan officer knows that most mortgage loan applicants may be a bit anxious about the process and he or she should do everything possible to answer the applicant's questions. The applicant should take as much time as needed to ask questions about financing desires that may not have been put forth by the loan officer. A loan officer that takes the time to answer the applicant's questions is one sign of a loan officer more willing to help meet an applicant's needs and act as an advisor in the transaction.

Many of the questions an applicant has can be answered during the initial interview over the telephone. If the applicant is not comfortable with the performance of the loan officer because of any of the items listed above, the conclusion of the initial meeting may be that it is time to quickly select another loan officer or lending company. It may be too late to make a change later down the road.

It is incumbent upon the loan officer to analyze the data collected during the face-to-face interview. The loan officer is not there just to collect documents. In fact, the loan officer should attempt to identify and discuss any problems that may arise based upon his review. Whether identifying the applicant's individual constraints is accomplished during the telephone interview or in person, it is a necessary part of the process.

Lenders weight the demonstrated willingness and ability of a potential borrower to meet the debt service of the loan along with continuing to meet the debt service on other loans and credit cards. The ability to pay is a fairly rigid borrower constraint. An applicant earns what an applicant earns. While there are guidelines as to the ratio of the projected monthly mortgage payment to the applicant's gross stable monthly income, one cannot alter the applicant's income with explanation letters. However, the applicant's demonstrated ability to meet off-standard debt to income ratios bodes well in the underwriting of the loan. Understand that the projected monthly mortgage payment, which includes principal, interest, taxes and insurance, is, to a large extent, interest rate and loan term driven. While an applicant may desire a 15-year fixed rate mortgage, the payment may be too great to permit approval as it could push the applicants debt-to-income ratio well beyond that accepted by many lenders. Changing the loan term to 30-years, thus lowering the mortgage payment and placing the applicant back into the standard debt-to-income range may solve this problem. In most cases borrowers have the option to make larger payments which causes the debt to be retired prior to the scheduled loan term. Adjustable interest rate loans generally have lower starting note rates when compared to their fixed rate brethren. To avoid perceived payment shock, many lenders qualify the borrower using the projected interest rate after the first adjustment period. Even using this calculation, the first adjustment rate is very often less than a fixed rate loan. A word of caution here, adjustable rate mortgage loans should not be offered without the applicant clearly understanding its behavioral characteristics. An applicant on a fixed income or whose costs of living may rise significantly should be offered an adjustable rate mortgage loan only after using extreme caution, and insuring that he fully understands the operation of this loan type.

Some self-employed applicants are unable to accurately document their stable monthly income for various reasons including the complex nature of their tax returns. For those applicants, the no-income verification loan may be the avenue to pursue, understanding that what lenders give up in the verification of income end of underwriting, they often offset in higher home equity requirements, higher required credit scores and increased interest rates.

The applicant's credit history is another potential constraint with which one may have to deal. Poor past credit performance is a key hindrance to the approval process. In some cases a loan approval is still possible when logical explanations for credit problems are asserted. This kind of approval may be coupled with reduced loan-to-value ratios and possibly higher than standard interest rates. Erroneous items on an applicant's credit report that negatively impact the credit standing or credit score should be corrected as quickly as possible.

The amount of debt the applicant possesses at the time of application is a constraint. In a purchase transaction, this may be difficult to overcome unless the applicant has other liquid assets that can be utilized to both pay for the down payment and closing costs on the home to be purchased, and contemporaneously eliminate some those debts having large monthly payments.

The third constraining element is the borrower's funds available to complete the purchase transaction. If an applicant presently owns a home which will be sold, the cash available from that sale will be based upon the sum of the sales price of the home, less the outstanding balance on mortgages existing, less closing costs. Those funds, coupled with other liquid assets, must be calculated into the transaction. Lenders do not like to grant the loan request where a total depletion of cash reserves is involved. In refinance transactions this problem is generally eliminated as the closing costs can be financed into the new loan.

The source document from which all other information will flow is that of the mortgage loan application form, referred to in the industry as the 1003 or "Ten-Oh-Three." The 1003 is nothing more than a financial statement containing various schedules. The form may not be in the format many are used to but it is, in fact, a financial statement. It lists assets, liabilities, and net worth; it is dated and signed; it has schedules as to real estate assets owned and debts due.

Section I of the form lays out the type of mortgage loan being applied for and its terms. This section is fairly self-explanatory asking for the amount of the loan request, whether the applicant is looking for a fixed rate loan or an adjustable rate loan, the interest rate being requested and the term of the loan requested.

Section II of the form delves into the purpose of the loan and the property to be financed. Is the purpose of the loan a purchase of a new home or a refinance of an existing property? Will the property be the owner-occupied primary residence, a second home, or is the applicant looking to finance an investment property. Lastly, this section attempts to determine in whose name the property will be held and the source of the down-payment and costs to complete the loan transaction.

The last two sections of the first page of the application list questions pertaining to personal data of the applicants. Section III questions include the applicants' ages, present addresses, dates of birth, length of time at the current address and whether the applicants currently own or rent the property in which they reside. Section IV relates to questions regarding the applicants' employment. In these two sections, it is important that applicants provide a full two-year history. Anything less could cause a delay in processing.

The second page of the 1003 deals with the applicants' monthly income from all sources along with the applicants' current housing expense. This page also asks the applicants to list their assets, both liquid and non-liquid along will all debts. Summary line items include bank deposits, stocks and bonds held, the current value of retirement funds along with tangible assets such as automobiles. The sum of the liabilities is subtracted from the sum of the assets to derive a Net Worth figure.

Beginning in Section V on Page 2 of the 1003, a detail of the applicant's income is required. This section contains the following line items: Base Employment Income; Overtime; Bonuses; Commissions; Dividends/Interest; Net Rental Income, and; Other Income. Remembering that lenders consider "Stable Monthly Income" as the basis for debt service, non-recurring items are generally excluded from consideration. Therefore, applicants that received bonus or overtime income in the past but may not receive the income in the future will usually not be able to use that income to qualify.

The final page contains Sections VI through X. Section VI is the schedule of Real Estate presently owned and debts and costs associated with each property. The sum of this schedule must match the summary lines of real estate owned and mortgage liability on the second page. The loan officer should be the person to complete the Details of Transaction while the applicant can complete the Declarations and Acknowledgment and Agreement Sections of the 1003. It is very important, critical in fact, that the applicants sign and date the application form. The Government Monitoring Information questions below the signature lines must also be completed. If the applicant does not wish to furnish the information, the loan officer is required to complete the information to the best of his ability. This section is needed to insure that no single protected class of applicant is treated less favorably than other classes of applicants.

If the loan officer was successful in obtaining enough information at the time of the telephone interview and had the applicant's permission, he was probably able to obtain a credit report and complete the liability section of the application before ever meeting with the applicants. Obtaining the missing pieces at the time of the face-to-face interview is the only remaining step needed to finish the qualification process. Once the application is compete, the loan officer will be able to calculate the debt-to-income ratio on the mortgage loan and the ratio for continuing obligations to see if the applicant continues to fit into the general guidelines for the loan plan they have requested. Many successful loan officers are able to hand deliver a written loan approval to the applicant after the face-to-face interview by first obtaining information at the time of the telephone interview and obtaining approval utilizing an automated underwriting system of Federal National Mortgage Association or the Federal Home Loan Mortgage Corporation (Fannie Mae and Freddie Mac, respectively). There is nothing more powerful for a loan officer than to complete the face-to-face interview by handing a loan approval documents to the applicants.

Different lenders may have other forms they require the applicants to sign at the time of the application, including a credit authorization form, interest rate lock-in form and acknowledgments of receipt of other disclosure forms. If the loan officer was able to issue a written approval at the time of application, the applicant should seek a narrative of the step-by-step course of action to be taken on the applicant's loan processing, concluding with the loan closing and a realistic time frame for meeting the requirements of each step.

Traps

There are built in "traps" to the 1003 that can stumble a borrower. When these traps are understood by the applicant, or skillfully negotiated by the loan officer, the process of obtaining a loan approval can be expedited.

The Title Trap - There are three traps in Section II of the 1003.

The first is the Title Trap. The Title Trap occurs when the property will be titled differently than in the names of the applicants. If the property will be titled in a different fashion than that which is reflected on the loan application, a problem will arise. By way of example, if John Doe is applying for the mortgage loan and John, in answer to the question, "How will the property be titled" replies, "Phil and Mary Smith," and the loan officer asks no further questions, a trap has been set. Without further explanations, the applicant and loan officer leave themselves open to a major problem that may not be recognized until the loan is being set up for closing. Being told that there is a problem with the loan just after loading the contents of an existing home on a moving van places everyone involved in an unpleasant position. The applicant and the loan officer must pause in the application process to ascertain the relationship between these people. Depending upon that relationship between the applicant and the persons to be named in title, some state laws may prevail and require signatures on at least the mortgage or deed of trust documents. Additionally, if the applicant is a non-occupying co-borrower, the loan-to-value ratio may be affected. In most cases, while a lender may not require a spouse to become an obligor on the Note, even if the applicant is married, some states require that the both spouses sign the property related documents such as the mortgage, trust deed or deed in order to effect a proper and enforceable lien.

The second trap is the Source of Down-Payment Trap. This, too, can be a deal killer. Suppose the applicant indicates that the source of down payment and settlement costs will come from savings accounts on hand. Later in the application process, the applicant states that he has $15,000 on deposit. Now suppose that toward the end of the process, while calculating the Details of Transaction, the loan officer arrives at a figure of $20,000 for cash to close. If the applicant and the loan officer just fill in the blanks on the form and do not reconcile these three questions, they will be caught in the Source of Down Payment Trap. As soon as it is realized that the applicant has a source of funds less than the requirement needed to complete the transaction, this information should be brought to light and solutions sought. The applicant may have missed listing deposit accounts, retirement accounts or gifts that the applicant will be receiving from relatives, on the application form. Deposit statements provided by the applicant should be examined closely, insuring that sufficient sources of funds indeed exist.

The Commission Income Trap - When completing the income section of the 1003, stated commission should alert the applicant and loan officer to a documentation follow-up issue. The general rule is if the applicant's commission income is equal to or greater than 25% of the applicant's total employment income, tax returns may be a document requirement. Not supplying it at the time of application can be a problem later on in the processing phase of the loan.

There are at least two common traps on Page 3 of the 1003. They include the Subordinate Financing Trap and the Seller-Paid Closing Costs Trap.

The Subordinate Financing Trap occurs when an applicant announces that he will be obtaining a second mortgage as part of his purchase plan. The approval the applicant is seeking may not permit subordinate financing. Additionally, the estimated monthly payment for the anticipated second mortgage must be included in the housing ratio which, when combined with the first mortgage and the monthly tax and insurance payment, may disqualify the applicant by increasing the housing ratio beyond that which is acceptable to the lender. It is imperative that the loan officer recalculates the applicant's ratios upon being advised that the applicant contemplates secondary financing. The loan officer must also review the underwriting guidelines to insure that the loan will be acceptable at the loan-to-value and the dollar amount of the down-payment the applicant is contemplating.

As in the case of the subordinate financing trap, the Seller-Paid Closing Costs Trap could make the difference between a loan being approved and a loan being rejected. The tricky part of this trap is it may not become apparent until it is too late. Many applicants fail to disclose that the person from whom they are purchasing the property is paying for some or all of the applicant's closing costs. This is especially critical in higher loan-to-value transactions. While the applicant may omit this information from the Details of Purchase section of the 1003, it is almost always disclosed in the purchase contract. Generally, lenders will not permit the third parties, including the seller, to contribute Seller-Paid Closing Costs amounting to more than a certain percentage of the loan amount, and almost never permit the so-called "prepaids" to be paid by someone other than the borrower. Prepaids include tax and insurance escrows along with prepaid interest. For lower loan-to-value loans, a six percent maximum third party payment of closing costs is generally permitted. The reason the lenders restrict the percentage of seller-paid closing costs is that at some point the parties to the purchase transaction will have to inflate the sales price to cover the additional out-of-pocket costs so as to net the seller the proceeds originally desired. The inflation of the sales price will negatively impact the lender in the event of borrower default and eventual foreclosure, as the lender will have to sell the home at market price upon its acquisition. If the market price was inflated, the lender may incur a larger loss upon resale. Loan officers must review the sales contract with an eye toward searching for any seller-paid contractual obligations that could affect the approval of the loan.

It is incumbent upon the loan officer to act as an advisor as opposed to just an application taker. As an example, suppose an applicant requests to refinance his existing home mortgage to take advantage of lower interest rates, without increasing the existing mortgage balance, with the exception of covering the closing costs. The applicant's first request may be to seek a 30-year fixed rate mortgage. The loan officer should review the remaining term on the existing loan.

Inquiry should also be made as to how long the applicant plans to live in the home. The answers may be surprising. If, for example, the applicant plans on moving to a smaller home once his children have finished school in a couple of years, a better alternative might be to suggest an adjustable interest rate loan product having an initial fixed rate period of three, five or seven years. The interest rates on these loans may be significantly lower than that of a 30-year fixed rate loan. By the time the first adjustment occurs, the borrowers will be out of the home. This planning may save the applicants thousands of dollars and the applicants may never have considered this alternative without benefit of the loan officer's wisdom.

Consider the case of significant credit card and other revolving debt coupled with below standard savings rates. A homeowner may benefit from a cash-out refinance for use as both an interest rate reduction and a debt consolidation loan. In many cases, credit card interest rates may be much higher than that of the residential mortgage. The reduction in monthly payment by the elimination of recurring credit card payments, coupled with the reduction in the interest rate of the applicant's existing mortgage loan, may afford the applicant the ability to begin moving the now increased disposable income into savings. It is strongly suggested that in any debt consolidation loan the bulk of the revolving credit card accounts be closed, not just paid off.

Suppose an applicant wishes a no cash-out loan to reduce the current interest rate on his loan. In the process of taking the application the loan officer discovers that the applicant plans on remaining in his home for the rest of his remaining life. The applicant has also requested a zero point loan. After considering all of the data available, a good loan officer may wish to mention to the applicant that a much lower interest rate is available coupled with the payment of loan fees used to "buy-down" the rate quoted. A calculation of the increased costs associated with a bought-down interest rate, divided by the reduction in monthly principal and interest payment over the market interest rate, will provide a break-even analysis. If, for example, it will take twenty-four months to reach the break-even point, and the applicant plans on living in the home for at least the next ten years, the buy-down of the interest rate will save the applicant a weighty sum of money. The applicant may have never considered paying a fee for a lower interest rate, but showing the applicant that the payment of a fee for a lower rate, and the long-term savings accompanying the lower rate, may be a very welcomed suggestion.

Analyzing the applicant's financial statement, the 1003, coupled with the listening to what the applicant is saying, enables a loan officer to become an advisor rather than just an application taker. Remember, the applicant must be comfortable with the advice the loan officer is providing so that in the final analysis, the loan officer guides and advises rather than insisting. What may be simple to an experienced loan officer may be more complex to the non-mortgage professional.

The Closing Process
by
Marilyn Hevia

The closing process is ready to commence once the borrower receives a loan commitment from the lender and all title issues are addressed. All underwriting conditions requested by the loan committee should have been cleared by this time. It is the closing department in a mortgage production company who has the final responsibility for transitioning the loan from processing and underwriting through the preparation, execution, funding, and shipping of the loan. Within this broad scope of responsibilities there are numerous functions to be performed including compliance checks, preparation and review of documents, review of property and title insurance, and funding.

The number of ways in which these functions are organized within a production organization are as varied as the number of mortgage companies originating loans. Ultimately, they are designed to accomplish the same objective.

When the loan file is sent to the closing department certain policies and procedures are put in place to ensure a valid lien position for the lender and to ensure the marketability of the loan. The closer verifies that the conditions on the loan commitment have been met and reviews the loan for legal and underwriting compliance.

The closing itself will usually be conducted by a settlement agent. Many times a title company serves in this capacity, and often times the attorney for either the seller or buyer fulfills this role. It is the closer's responsibility to interact with the agent and to prepare the approved loan for closing. The closing process involves various reviews and inspections. In clearing the required conditions as outlined in the loan commitment, certain procedures should be followed.

Review and Analysis

When reviewing the loan commitment, the closer will ensure that the closing is structured in accordance with the final loan approval and the individual loan program description. Certain items are checked at this point for accuracy including basic information such as names and addresses. Determining who will sign the note and mortgage and who will be on title to the property is as important as qualifying for the loan. Establishing how the parties will take title to the property depends on their own personal preference, underwriting rules, and the legal ramifications. Borrowers having any questions or doubt on this issue should consult an attorney.

The lender's commitment outlines the terms of the loan approval including loan amount, loan program, repayment terms and any outstanding items necessary to close the loan. This information is vital in establishing which closing forms will be used for the individual loan. Requirements such as inspection reports, property insurance, survey, escrows, and clear title insurance are examples of outstanding conditions that can be found on a loan commitment. Although all of these items are shown as requirements for the borrower to comply with prior to closing, the settlement agent should also be advised of these conditions prior to the preparation of the final closing documents. Providing the agent with a copy of the loan commitment sometimes serves as a tool for obtaining outstanding items. Different involved parties such as the realtor, seller, mortgage broker, developer, and the closing agent often assist the borrower by arranging to secure the services of reputable companies who perform the inspections and reports required.

Within a reasonable period of time prior to closing, a Standard Flood Hazard Determination Form is requested by the lender to determine if the property is located within a designated flood hazard area and if federal flood insurance is available. A "Notice of Special Flood Hazards and Availability of Federal Disaster Relief Assistance" disclosure is provided to the borrower. This disclosure advises the borrower if the community in which the property is located participates in the National Flood Insurance Program and relates the particular requirements for the purchase of the insurance. Both the determination form and a copy of the signed disclosure should be kept as part of the borrower's file throughout the life of the loan.

In the event that flood insurance is required, a flood insurance policy must be purchased together with a homeowners hazard insurance policy. The loan commitment will outline the exact requirements of these insurances.

Arrangements to purchase homeowners and flood insurance policies are made by the borrower prior to the date of the settlement and should be in effect on the closing date. Payment of premiums can be arranged at closing or paid for in advance according to the insurance agent's requirements. Nonetheless, paid receipts for the first year of coverage will likely be required at closing. Some lenders require that subsequent payments of hazard and flood insurance be the responsibility of the loan servicer and collect one twelfth of the total yearly premium as part of the borrowers monthly payment.

The amount of coverage required is usually equal to the loan amount, the replacement value of the property or the maximum amount available. Replacement value is determined by subtracting the land value from the total value of the property as shown on the property appraisal.

Under certain circumstances, if the lender feels that adequate coverage has not been obtained, they will require that the policy specify that full replacement coverage is in place. The policies must specify that the lender is a loss payee. Some regions of the country require that additional insurances be purchased to cover specific hazardous conditions such as hurricanes and earthquakes.

When the property being financed is a condominium unit, the property insurance is typically handled by the homeowners association. Certain developments known as Planned Unit Developments can also fall into this category depending on how the property was initially platted. In these circumstances, when a homeowner pays his monthly maintenance, the coverage for hazard and flood insurance is included. A copy of the master policy's declaration (dec) page is required for the borrowers file. The 'dec' sheet must name the particular unit owner and reference the unit number, and must also name the lender as the loss payee. Ideally, the expiration date should be for a minimum of one year. When determining if the coverage is adequate, many lenders will divide the total number of units in the condominium building by the total coverage amount. If the resulting number is less than the loan amount, showing full replacement cost on the 'dec' sheet is sometimes sufficient to satisfy most lenders. It is not uncommon, however, to have lenders require that homeowners who fall into this category of ownership purchase individual policies as well.

The Settlement Agent and Title Insurance

The settlement agent is generally chosen at time of application by the borrower unless agreed upon in advance by both parties involved in a purchase transaction. Although the closing is handled at an organization chosen by the borrower, the settlement agent must be approved by the lender and must provide the lender indemnification documentation in the form of a closing protection letter and a copy of their errors and omissions policy.

The settlement agent is responsible to and represents the lender at closing and must fully comply with all of the closing instructions received from the lender. He will be in charge of all disbursement of monies as disclosed on the settlement statement to the applicable parties. The closing agent is responsible for complying with all federal truth in lending laws, the Real Estate Settlement Procedures Act (RESPA) and any other state or federal laws.

The closer for the lender coordinates the timely delivery of a complete closing package to the settlement agent and arranges for the funding of the loan. It is best that this process is completed in a timely manner in advance of the closing to ensure a smooth transaction and allow the borrower time to review the documents and settlement statement. Final arrangements for the cash to close will be made by the borrower.

Prior to the loan reaching the closer, a title search of the property is done by the settlement agent and a title binder issued to the lender. A search is necessary to determine if there are any defects or encumbrances on title and to prevent fraudulent sales. The search indicates any outstanding liens, judgments, encroachments, easements, outstanding oil and mineral rights, and all covenants and conditions. Schedule B-1 of the title commitment (also known as a title binder) outlines the requirements which the closing agent must clear in order to insure good and marketable title. The gap, the survey and the mechanic's lien exceptions are forms of "general exceptions" that the agent will be required to delete from the final title insurance policy. Affidavits are obtained by the closing agent to eliminate liens and ensure that all outstanding loans are subordinate to the lender's. Once the final title commitment is issued, all of the requirements should have been deleted and only acceptable exceptions should remain. Schedule B-II outlines the exceptions which will remain permanently on the final title policy. Acceptable exceptions may vary among different investors but ultimately serve the same purpose, to provide the lender with clear, marketable title and the agreed upon lien position. Frequently appearing and approved by investors are exceptions relative to easements created by utility companies. The easements are set up to run along one or more of the sides of the property. Any encroachments onto the property reflected on the survey will appear as exceptions and should be approved by the lender. City taxes for the year in which a loan is being closed and are not yet due show as an acceptable exception. The exceptions on the title binder should read exactly as they will on the final title policy once the binder has been delivered to the lender. After all the permanent exceptions are listed, the binder should specify which endorsements will be included in the final title policy as applicable to the specific loan. The lender will review and approve the title binder before closing.

Schedule A of the binder includes the legal description of the property, the dollar amount of insurance, and the names of the borrowers as they will appear on the title. The legal description must be exactly the same on the mortgage, the survey and the deed.

A property survey is required when the property being financed is a single family dwelling. The property can be detached or attached as a part of a planned unit development. The survey is primarily utilized to identify the property boundaries and indicate the dimensions and location of the easements, shows all of the improvements, any encroachments onto the property, and determines any zoning or plat violations. All easements and encroachments should be reflected identically on the survey and the title insurance commitment. Any violation or encroachment will be listed as an exception on the title commitment and should be approved by the lender. The survey re-certifies the legal description and property address. The survey also shows what flood zone the property is in and indicates which flood map was used in determining it. An original survey containing a raised seal traditionally forms part of the lenders file and is certified to all of the involved parties in the transaction including the title company, the lender, and the borrowers. Obtaining a survey allows the settlement agent to delete the survey exception from the title commitment. It is up to the lender to approve exceptions obtained from the survey.

Any required inspection reports should be completed, reviewed and approved by the lender before the preparation of the closing documents. If the lender discovers any unacceptable damage to the property through the inspection reports, he may choose to require that repairs be completed in a satisfactory manner prior to closing. The lender will usually allow sufficient time prior to closing for the borrower or the seller to complete the repairs to the property or on occasion, will allow that monies be held in escrow by the closing agent for an agreed period of time after closing to facilitate the completion. It is at the sole discretion of the lender as to how to handle the disbursement of the escrow funds.

Document Preparation

Among the numerous tasks asked of the closing agent, specific information is provided to them regarding the loan amount, interest rate, payment amount, and loan program to facilitate the explaining of each document to the borrower during the closing. An itemized list of the documents being sent for signature is included with the closing instructions. All documents are rechecked for accuracy and correctness.

The closer prepares the documents to be sent to the closing agent for execution. Unless an investor has its own form for legal documentation, the standard Fannie Mae/Freddie Mac forms will usually be utilized for closing.

Typed Loan Application

A typed loan application is the final version of the handwritten application submitted by the borrower when applying for mortgage financing. By signing this document at closing, the borrower restates the information initially provided to the lender and confirms its authenticity. He is also acknowledging the final terms of the loan which have been incorporated into the application such as the interest rate, the monthly payment amount, cash to close, and terms of the loan, making the application complete.

HUD-I Settlement Statement

The settlement statement is considered to be the most important document at the closing by some borrowers due to the financial impact of the transaction as a whole. It expresses the reality of the cost of borrowing money by itemizing all the fees charged by all the parties involved in the transaction. The settlement agent is provided with a list of charges to be collected and specific instructions about how these charges should be reflected on the HUD-I. All monies to be collected for interest and escrows are identified in detail. The lender should always review and approve the HUD-I before it is executed. A representative of the title company will sign the settlement statement as confirmation that all of the fees have been reviewed and accepted by all parties.

Note - (also known as Promissory Note)

The promissory note is the legal document executed by all parties obligated to repay the debt. Borrowers are provided with detailed information necessary to repay the debt relative to their loan program. The particular terms are spelled out clearly to the borrower including the loan amount, interest rate and monthly principal and interest payments. The note reflects the address of where the monthly payments are to be sent, when the first payment is due and when the loan will mature. Grace periods and late charges are disclosed according to applicable investor requirements and state law.

Mortgage- (Deed of Trust in some locations)

The mortgage or Deed of Trust is the legal instrument which encumbers the property with the lenders interest and is recorded in the public records of the county in which the property is located. Also referred to as a lien, it will be in place until the loan is paid in full at which time a Satisfaction of Mortgage or Satisfaction of Deed of Trust will be recorded. Although the terms of financing are re-established on the mortgage, a broader scope of conditions and home ownership responsibilities are also provided ranging from specific property maintenance requirements, adequate insurance coverage, and the governing laws of the state in which the property is located. Transfer of title to the property, default on monthly payments and other specific circumstances are addressed as possibilities for creating a default under the mortgage. The right of the lender to foreclose on the property is also explained.

Final TIL Disclosure

The Truth-in-Lending Act applies only in certain circumstances. Commercial loans for example are exempt from this disclosure and some investors view loans being taken on investment property as being commercial loans, therefore, not requiring the disclosure. Lending institutions typically choose to provide the disclosure nonetheless because of its significance. The TIL outlines the annual percentage rate of borrowed money taking into consideration certain fees incurred for the purpose of obtaining a mortgage loan. These fees include points, underwriting and processing fees to name a few. They are also referred to as Prepaid Finance Charges.

Payment Letter

A payment letter is provided to the borrower at closing itemizing exactly the monthly payment the borrower will be required to pay, the date on which the first payment is due, to whom the payments are to be made, and where they are to be sent.

Miscellaneous Documents

The complete package that is sent to the closing agent for execution may contain other miscellaneous documents according to specific investor requirements. Some of these include a compliance agreement, escrow disclosure and property tax information request.

Funding

Arrangements to fund the loan are set in place in accordance with prior arrangements made between the closing agent and the lender.

Fundings can take place through the use of bank checks, bank warehouse drafts and electronic wires.

Post Closing

The post closing department handles the final process of the closing by seeing the loan through to shipping and servicing of the loan.

Warehousing

Of utmost importance and priority is ensuring that the funding check clears without difficulty when the loan proceeds sent to the closing agent are from a warehousing line of credit through a banking institution. Certain documents must be provided to the bank to be used as collateral including the original promissory note endorsed in blank and an assignment of mortgage in recordable form. Requirements from different banks vary but the concept is similar. In accordance with procedures set up in advance, either the lender or the warehouse bank will deliver the security instruments to the final investor with instructions for repayment of the warehouse line.

Auditing

Closed loan packages are received together with the lender's fees and escrow monies if applicable. The post closer verifies that all the disbursements are accurate and in accordance with the lender's closing instructions and the HUD-I. All documents are checked for accuracy, consistency, and completeness. A crosscheck of the legal description with the mortgage or deed of trust and title policy is made, and signatures on all the required documents are checked.

Shipping

Frequently when a lender closes a loan, he does so with the intention of selling the loan to another investor. The decision of who the investor will be is sometimes determined as early as at the time of the loan application. The originator selects the program which best fits the borrower's needs and tailors the loan in accordance with the investor's requirements. At closing the lender will provide the settlement agent with an assignment of mortgage to the final investor to have that assignment recorded in the Public Records. Once the investor has purchased the loan, the transaction is complete.

Wiring instructions are provided to the investor with the package so that the warehousing bank is paid off directly. Once the loan has been purchased by the investor, the borrowers will be notified of any changes made from their previous arrangements involving their monthly payments. Insurance agents are also notified of any changes, especially if the loan will be serviced by someone other than the initial lender who closed the loan.

Recorded Documents

As a final check the auditor makes certain that all recorded documents, including mortgages, trust deeds, assignments, and the final title insurance policies are received and reviewed for accuracy. These original final documents are incorporated into the borrowers file or forwarded to the investor, finalizing the post closer's and the closing department's responsibility with the loan.

Borrower Beware!
by
Patrick Mansell

The discussion of how to save on closing costs and avoid the pitfalls of overpaying for closing services begins with an analysis of what closing costs are or should be. The subject is of utmost importance to any individual about to embark on a new mortgage loan whether it is a purchase money first or second mortgage, or a refinance of existing debt. Because regulation of unscrupulous practices is difficult, if not impossible to administer, an entire industry has grown and become a part of the seedy side of the mortgage lending business. The states and federal authorities have been mostly ineffective in enforcing the regulations that have been promulgated to protect mortgage consumers. Therefore it is up to the consumer to protect himself.

Anyone who has ever been a party to a mortgage loan closing transaction knows that the cost of home financing is not inexpensive. The litany of closing costs seems to go on and on, and fills up the entire second page of a closing statement (HUD 1). While the lender and closing agent might seem to be nickel and dimeing the borrower to death, most charges are necessary and unavoidable. Comparing one mortgage to another is not as simple as comparing only rates and points. Borrowers need to shop other components of the mortgage transaction including rates, points and fees. Some costs can range from being reasonable, to being somewhat out of line, to being vastly overcharged. By knowing when costs are excessive a borrower can position himself to avoid overpaying. Many closing costs are flexible or negotiable, many others are not.

The typical borrower who qualifies for a loan that conforms to the requirements of "A" grade investment quality paper is in a position to negotiate fees simply because there are so many lenders and brokers who will compete for his business. The market for investment quality loans is highly organized and liquid. Money flows into that market by the billions of dollars each day. The mortgage lender or broker who holds himself out as doing an "A" quality borrower a favor by being able to place his loan, is not being entirely honest with that borrower. In such a case a borrower can expect lenders and brokers to compete on the basis of cost and service to get that loan. In states where documentary stamps, recording fees and other surcharges and surtaxes are collected, there should be no expectation of being able to negotiate those fees.

Lenders frequently change loan terms between the time of the loan application and closing. There are often legitimate reasons for doing so, but there are also many times when there are not. It is therefore suggested that an applicant monitor every step in the process to avoid costs they are not expecting or can not afford to pay. If this language serves to upset or scare a potential applicant, then that is a good thing. The financing of a home is the largest money transaction most people will face in their lifetime, and if fear is what it takes to get a borrower's attention and have him/her fully analyze the transaction and the risks associated with it, then to be forewarned is to be forearmed.

One of the ways that mortgage brokers and lenders hide fees is by using terminology that is unfamiliar to a borrower. The lender may quote 'no points' and 'no origination fee'. A borrower might take comfort in knowing that he has a zero points, zero origination fee loan only to find out later that the broker or lender is charging a discount on the mortgage, which is in effect another way of charging points. In the initial disclosure documents provided to the borrower it is quite possible that this eventuality was noted, but it would be a very easy thing to miss when applying for the loan. A borrower should ask at the time of the application about points, origination fees, broker fees and discounts. It would be a good idea to also have the loan officer who takes the application point out where in the disclosure documents it states that there are no such charges. Usually if such costs are to be charged they will appear either on the Good Faith Estimate, the Mortgage Brokerage Agreement, or the initial TIL (Truth In Lending Disclosure). It is important to note that it is possible to go all the way through the loan origination process without ever receiving notice that a discount is to be charged. A mortgage lender could, under these circumstances, instruct the closing agent to charge a discount to the borrower that is to be paid at closing. In this event the borrower would not have found out about the additional charge until perhaps a few days before closing. As closings go, borrowers are vulnerable in these last few days because they may be in a position where closing is an absolute necessity and they have left themselves no other option than to close this loan with this lender. An applicant is well advised to read and be familiar with all the terms of the mortgage agreement by cross referencing the initial disclosure documents with the lock-in agreement, when applicable, and by obtaining a separate statement from the broker or lender that only those fees as enumerated on the Good Faith Estimate will be charged. It is not difficult to envision a situation whereby a mortgage broker or lender will refuse to close the loan unless these additional fees are paid. In addition to covering one's self from the outset with the disclosure documentation, a borrower should also check references and look into the credibility and trustworthiness of the lender to whom he is applying.

Discounts and Premiums

Aside from out of pocket expenses incidental to the closing, some of which are actual expenses of the loan, others of which are sometimes referred to as 'junk fees', the lender compensation on the loan itself will be derived from a combination of points (whether referred to as originations fees, points, or discounts) and the interest rate charged. On the sale of the loan in the secondary mortgage market, the originator will be paid a percentage of the loan amount depending upon the quality of the loan and the interest rate the note carries. That percentage can be more than, equal to, or less than the face amount of the loan. When an investor pays less than the face amount of the loan that is said to be discounted. When an investor pays dollar for dollar the exact amount of the loan, he is said to be paying par for the loan. And when the investor pays more for the loan than its face amount that is called paying a premium. With this background, it can be seen that the originator of the loan might charge no origination fees, no points and no discount, but might still have an opportunity to market the loan at a premium and in that way book profits. In a more typical example the originator of the loan would charge some kind of points to the borrower and also charge the investor in the loan a premium to sell the loan to him. Not that this is a bad thing, it is just important background to have when deciding how to proceed with a lender.

Locking-In

An important consideration with respect to rate and points is whether or not to lock in the interest rate at the time of application or to allow the rate to float. To float the rate during the time of processing and leading up to the closing is neither a good thing or a bad thing, it is simply a matter of deciding if the rate being offered at the time of application, in combination with the closing fees agreed to in advance, are satisfactory. As a heads up, very often applicants who decide they will allow the rate to float will be hit with the bad news that rates have gone up during time the loan application was in process, and they are now facing a higher interest rate than they had expected when they applied. The are three possible reasons why this has happened to the applicant. The first and most legitimate cause is because interest rates actually did go up during the time the loan was in process. This happens with approximately the same frequency as rates going down during the time the loan was in process. The second reason is because the lender or broker is using this as a ploy to sell the higher yielding loan to an investor for a greater premium. The third reason is because this is the way the originator of the loan does his business, meaning he lures his customers in with a vague promise of a lower rate at the time of application and later hits him with the news that his rate will be higher at closing because the interest rate market moved against the applicant during the time between the loan application and closing. As mentioned earlier, these possibilities are out there for every mortgage applicant to consider, and nailing down the details of the interest rates and points is of prime importance.

Junk Fees

Mention was made earlier of what is referred to in the mortgage industry as 'junk fees'. This is an ugly term for additional charges that a lender or broker might charge in addition to the interest rate, points, origination fees and discounts. Included in this category are documentation preparation fees, funding fees, warehousing fees, processing fees, underwriting fees and inspection fees. It can not be said with a certainty that these fees are unnecessary or that they are merely charged to add to the profits of the loan originator. Nor can it be said that they are not. Each originator of mortgage loans has different ways of having services provided, and each of the fees enumerated above can have a place in the overall loan process. As an example, one fee that is often charged on a closing is for documentation preparation, referred to as a 'doc prep' fee. The fact is that some lenders prepare their own closing documents with in-house software and their out of pocket expense for this is nil. Others who prepare their own documents may use another vendor's software for which they have an offsetting expense to the doc prep fee. Likewise, an underwriting fee might be charged in a situation where the underwriting of the loan is done in-house at no additional expense to the lender, while another may actually have an out of pocket expense for underwriting because they use third party contract underwriters or automated underwriting engines for which a fee is charged.

The Tricks of the Good Faith Estimate

Even borrowers who shop diligently for the right loan with the right lender can be misled by the disclosures given at the time of application. The Good Faith Estimate is a disclosure that was promulgated through the Department of Housing and Urban Development, the watchdog federal agency that was established in part to protect the rights of mortgage borrowers. Under the Real Estate Settlement and Procedures Act (RESPA) the requirement was established that mortgage lenders and brokers in a residential mortgage transaction must provide the applicant with an estimate of closing costs. This Good Faith Estimate (GFE) is intended to inform the applicant of all closing costs that will be incurred on behalf of the lender in the loan transaction. While this should give comfort to the applicant that he is protected by these disclosures, there are simply too many areas where an unscrupulous mortgage lender or broker can under-disclose or fail to disclose without fear of reprisal or legal action.

A mortgage applicant may use an abundance of caution and sit down with a number of different lenders to compare closing cost estimates before committing to one of them to be the service provider. The applicant would have to be very astute to catch the subtle differences between the various estimates, and may select a lender because his rates and costs appear most competitive only to find out that the lender has either under-disclosed certain items or left other items completely out.

As an example, in order to make his closing costs look favorable, a loan officer might estimate that title insurance will be $350 as compared to another lender's estimate of $1,200. The applicant might conclude that the first estimate is $850 lower than the second and be compelled to go with that lender. The fact is that title insurance is not an expense of the lender, it is a charge of the title company or attorney providing the closing services and title insurance. The lender who provided the estimate for $350 is not bound by that estimate as it is not a cost that is incurred on the lender's behalf. It is fallacious to think that the first lender's costs are lower just because he gave a lower estimate for title insurance.

Another area where costs can appear out of line has to do with estimated prepaid interest and escrows. An estimate for daily interest may be calculated and disclosed as a single day's interest by one lender while another lender's estimate may show 30 days of interest. The first lender's estimate is going to look better because of this, but it in no way means that his costs are lower. While a hazard policy may be a lender requirement, it is an expense attributable to the insurance company, not the lender. In a typical transaction a lender would want the policy paid a year in advance plus a two month's cushion of premiums in the escrow account. One lender's estimate might cover the entire fourteen months of hazard insurance while another's might not estimate for it at all making his estimate look much better than the one with the full disclosure.

These tricks of the Good Faith Estimate are not always innocent errors. They are frequently calculated to mislead the applicant into a sense that one transaction is less expensive than another. A prudent borrower will not only compare these estimates and find out the basis for the differences, but will also seek the advice of an expert in these matters if the facts remain unclear.

There are many thousands of mortgage lenders operating within the United States. In fact there are thousands of mortgage lenders including brokers, finance companies, banks, credit unions, and savings banks operating in every state. This leaves the field wide open for consumers to make choices with respect to what resource they want to use to handle their mortgage transaction. Before committing to a single lender for a loan, a borrower is well advised to thoroughly study the lender's proposal for financing, interview a number of lending sources, and check references. An honest lender or broker will be able to supply references from banks, Realtors, closing agents, and previous satisfied customers.

Mortgage Loan Servicing
by
Richard L. Higgins

In the field of mortgage banking, mortgage brokerage, and mortgage finance there are two distinct fields of expertise and two areas of the relationship to be understood by the borrower. The origination staff is that area of the mortgage banking organization that deals with marketing, pricing and underwriting. That staff takes the borrower from the application phase to the closing phase of the process. The second area of specialty for a borrower to understand and learn to deal with is mortgage servicing. Typically the mortgage originations area handles the client's loan for a period of several weeks, or in the extreme case, several months. The servicing area deals with the borrower for the rest of the time, the entire life of the loan until it is amortized or paid off. This can be a thirty year relationship.

The mortgage servicer serves two masters: the borrower, and the investor to whom the loan was sold. In the respect that any mortgage banker would want to retain its customers and encourage repeat business, it is in his interest to create a pleasant and workable relationship with his customer. That means handling the borrowers' payments expeditiously, applying payments accurately and in a timely manner, and maintaining error free records. An open line of communication between a servicing department and its customers is the surest way to maintain customers for life. And the second responsibility, no less important than the relationship with the customer, is the mortgage servicer's duty to the investor for whom he services mortgage loans.

The most basic responsibility a servicer has with respect to its borrower is the proper application of monthly payments to assure that the loan amortizes in accordance with the terms of the security instrument, more particularly the terms of the promissory note and its riders. In the instance of a fixed rate, fully amortizing mortgage, the servicer must make certain to apply all principal and interest payments in accordance with the established amortization schedule so that all sums are credited to the borrower as agreed, and the borrower is given full credit for principal and interest payments. In certain instances loan agreements have riders which set forth additional responsibilities for the borrower and conversely place additional responsibilities for the mortgage servicer to make certain that the riders are implemented in accordance with their terms. These riders to the note may take several forms, the most common of which is the Adjustable Rate Rider which sets forth the formula by which future interest rate changes will be applied. Another popular note rider is the Balloon Rider which sets forth the time in which all amounts under the note become due and payable, and which may also set forth additional terms under which the loan may be renewed at the balloon date. In addition to properly implementing these riders, the servicer also has the responsibility of notifying the borrower of these issues in a timely manner and in accordance with the terms of the note and riders.

Another function of the servicer, and one equally important as the application of payments under notes and riders, is the maintenance of borrowers' escrow accounts. Escrow accounts, commonly referred to as impounds, are established as an additional protection for the lender or investor. Monthly payments may be collected for a variety of reasons, but most commonly are for the payment of real estate taxes and insurance premiums. The reason that these two items are selected for escrow is that the payment of these amounts is so critical to the servicer's and investor's interest in the loan security. Because real estate taxes can create a lien superior to the mortgage lien, it is in the servicer's interest to collect the real estate taxes and make certain they are paid,

116

thus preserving its priority interest in the mortgaged property. Likewise, the lenders interest in the mortgaged premises can be threatened by the loss of value due to fire or storm damage. For this reason the servicer takes on the responsibility of ascertaining that insurance premiums are paid and policies do not lapse. These basic concepts create most of the servicer's work in that it must collect escrow payments, account for its disbursements, and maintain accurate records of all escrow transactions. Further, the servicer has an annual responsibility to analyze borrowers' escrow accounts, to provide a history of disbursements from that account, and give notice of the condition of that account.

The maintenance of escrow accounts is a moving target for mortgage servicers. The two main items for which monies are escrowed, real estate taxes and insurance premiums, rarely stay the same from year to year. When tax notices or insurance premium billings are received, the servicer must re-analyze the escrow account to be certain that the amounts collected are in balance with the amounts that will be needed to cover these expenses throughout the year. For this reason borrowers' monthly payments are subject to change from time to time. Unhappily, the payment for escrows rarely goes down, so notices from the servicer of escrow changes are not usually welcome.

There are times when escrow accounts accumulate surpluses. In such cases mortgage servicers are required to refund any amount greater than $50 over and above the amount required to meet anticipated expenses plus a cushion of two months. Frequently borrowers use their prerogative to apply this excess to pay down their mortgage balances.

As a part of maintaining escrow accounts for its borrowers, the mortgage servicer stays in contact with the mortgagors' insurance carriers. In addition to making certain that the carrier has correct billing instructions, the servicer also has itself named as additional loss payee on the policy and assists in the disbursement of insurance proceeds in the event of a claim. This procedure has the additional benefit of making certain that insurance premiums are paid on time and that there are no lapses in coverage.

The timely collection of mortgage payments from borrowers is a paramount responsibility of the mortgage servicer. While due dates and late charges can vary according to the terms of the security instrument, a typical scenario for collections might call for payments due on the first day of the month, with a grace period of ten days, and penalty charges accruing if the payment is received after the fifteenth of the month. In such a case, a mortgage servicer will send out a reminder notice at the end of the grace period and then follow that up with a late notice on the fifteenth. The late notice will also set forth the amount of the late charge that is due to be included in the payment. A note of caution here to all borrowers: so many times borrowers believe that because late charges do not accrue until the fifteenth, that the payment is not due until the fifteenth. This is fallacious and a very dangerous practice. Timing a payment so that it is received by the fifteenth can trip up the mortgagor, as a single day of delay in the postal service may cause the borrower to incur late charges. Payments due on the first of the month are due on the first, not the fifteenth.

The consequences of late payments or non-payments can have a damaging effect on a borrower's credit. To begin with, most servicers are required to report all payments more than thirty days past due to the credit reporting agencies. The loan is placed in a past due or delinquent status and the servicer then initiates more intense collection procedures. This may include sending registered collection letters, accelerating the loan, referring the collection to an attorney, or initiating foreclosure proceedings. In addition to the late charges accruing in such a scenario, the borrower might also incur additional expenses such as property inspections or attorney's fees.

At any time that a borrower falls behind in its mortgage obligation, the best course of action is to open a dialogue with the mortgage servicer. There are any number of ways that a servicer can assist a borrower who is having temporary financial problems that prevent him from making his scheduled payments. A skilled mortgage servicer will know of the various loss mitigation techniques that might include loan modification, stipulation, forbearance or a refinance. In the event that the financial difficulty is not temporary, a servicer might recommend the sale of the property as a preference to foreclosure. The sale will help free up the borrower's equity and possibly provide some cash after the sale. Foreclosure is a last resort as the borrowers will in most cases lose any hope of recovering cash from the equity in their home, will incur a great deal of legal expenses, and will ruin their credit for a long time to come.

With respect to tax reporting, the mortgage servicer must provide each borrower with a 1098 which states the amount of interest the borrower has paid throughout the year. This information is also provided to the Internal Revenue Service. Additionally, a statement of real estate taxes paid must be provided. This information is used in income tax filing as most mortgage interest and real estate taxes are deductible from federal income taxes.

A word of caution is provided here for new borrowers. Once a mortgage or deed of trust is recorded in the public records, the name and address of a borrower becomes public record. There are people and firms who make a living extracting information from these records, so it is quite likely that a new loan will generate a whole bunch of correspondence from solicitors. The name of the lender is also a matter of public record and many solicitations that are derived this way will use the name of the lender without permission, and the mailing will be made to appear to be from the lender. In the event that such solicitations are received and the nature of the mailing seems questionable or disturbing, it is always best to check with the lender to see if they have a legitimate interest in the product being offered. In most instances the answer will be that they have none.

In furtherance of the relationship between the borrower and servicer, for any borrower looking for additional financing, home equity financing, a new mortgage loan, or a refinance, the first place to look is the current servicer. Not only does that lender appreciate and cherish its borrowers as potential lifetime customers, it may be in a position to streamline the process based upon the information it already has in its files, or it may be in a position to modify the existing loan to the terms for which the borrower is looking. This inside track that an existing servicer enjoys not only can be a time saver for a borrower, but may also be a money saver as well. Both secondary market agencies, Fannie Mae and Freddie Mac, have programs whereby existing customers whose loans are owned by them can use a streamlined process to originate a refinance. This can save the borrower on costs such as appraisal and underwriting fees, while saving the lender a great deal of time and effort in processing documentation. These lender savings can be passed on the borrower in the way of reduced origination fees.

Along with the responsibilities to the borrower, the mortgage servicer has an equal responsibility to the investor or owner of the mortgage. Some lenders require the mortgage servicer to pass through the collection of principal and interest to them daily. Others may only require payment on a monthly basis. Either way, the mortgage servicer provides a monthly report of the principal and interest collections for each loan. He will then reconcile the payments that were made to the investor/owner.

There are two types of remittances that are the most popular. One is called actual/actual accounting whereby the lender passes through to the investor the actual amount that was collected during the month. The other is called scheduled/scheduled which is most commonly used when servicing Mortgage Backed Securities, and whereby the mortgage servicer guarantees the pass through of the scheduled principal and interest whether is was collected or not. If these amounts are advanced, the mortgage servicer is due those funds when collected. The reconciliations of these two various methods require the mortgage servicer to maintain an accurate set of books in order to balance the monies due to the investor/owner. In the case of Fannie Mae and Freddie Mac, who together account for the greatest number of residential mortgage loans, they perform their own accounting to balance to the mortgage servicer, and the servicer's accounts must be reconciled monthly. Any differences must be corrected prior to the next reporting cycle.

Most investors require the mortgage servicer to maintain an escrow account for each of their borrowers for the payment of taxes and insurances. Again, the investors require the mortgage servicer to account to them for the reconciliation of escrows being held for mortgages within their portfolio. This is usually done on a monthly basis. Once per year, a detailed audit is prepared for each investor to account for each borrowers escrow account.

When it comes to delinquent loans or loans that are in foreclosure, the mortgage servicer must notify the investor of what procedures are being taken to rectify any deficiencies in payments. A monthly report is sent to the investor outlining the steps taken since the last report. These steps include collection procedures, inspections made to the property, attorneys status of collection or foreclosure, and particular reports specifically required of the investor. Once the property is foreclosed, the investor is notified and will usually list the property with an experienced real estate agent for sale. In many cases there is enough equity in the property, or in some cases proceeds of default insurance, that the investor does not face a significant loss.

A mortgage servicer is measured on his performance with various investors, not only on his timely remittance of principal and interest, but how he handles the collection and foreclosure procedures. If payments are not received as scheduled, the investor hopes to receive the amount due to him including any missed payments at the time of sale of the foreclosed property.

Mortgage servicing is a more precise part of mortgage banking. Agencies such as Fannie Mae and Freddie Mac have guidelines to follow. These guides mostly regulate how the mortgage servicer will handle all of their servicing procedures for the agency and their institutional investors. A good mortgage servicer following these procedures will help minimize the risk in the investor's portfolio.

Part IV

Residential Real Estate

Valuation of Residential Real Estate
by
Joel B. Greenberg, SRPA

The appraisal of real estate has been a requirement for making a real estate mortgage loan since the Great Depression in the United States. The independent appraisal was determined by the United States Congress to be the best method to make sure that the lender was protected against losses due to foreclosures on over-priced real estate. The government has since promulgated its rules through the governmental agency, HUD (U.S. Dept. of Housing and Urban Development). It also created governmental loan programs under FHA (Federal Housing Administration) and VA (Veterans Administration). Fannie Mae and Freddie Mac were created to buy loans in the secondary market in order to place more money in circulation for lending on single family homes, and to reduce the risk of lenders losing money. These organizations then collateralize the loans in the bond market and that money is then used to fund new purchases of loans. In this way investors can spread their risk.

The appraisal industry has evolved over the years from the early days when the appraiser was expected to give an independent opinion of value with little or no regulation of the appraisal or the appraiser, to the present Uniform Standards of Professional Appraisal Practice known as USPAP, which governs the appraisal process and reporting methods. The latest major change in the Appraisal Regulations came out of the Savings and Loan crisis of the 1980's and early 1990's. A federal law was passed a law in 1989 to help the financial institutions recover from the approximate $500 billion in losses because of poor lending practices. The first impulse of the Congress was to regulate the appraisers who were initially blamed for these losses. After years of investigation, which included working through the bad loans and observing the actual loan documentation, the government realized that only a small percentage of the loses were due to poor appraisals. Most of the problems discovered were on account of lenders not following their own underwriting guidelines, which resulted in poor lending decisions.

One result of the federal investigation was a new law pertaining to appraisers. The Federal Regulation created the Appraisal Foundation, which oversees all appraisers by oversight of the 50 State Appraisal Boards. Originally it was determined that every loan over $50,000 which is funded, or may be funded, through a federally insured institution, must have an appraisal by a certified appraiser. The loan amount was later raised to $250,000. This change has had a dramatic effect on the appraisal profession and on the level of confidence a buyer can have in the value of his purchase. Since no appraisal is required for a large portion of the residential loans made, many houses are purchased without an appraisal or with the use of the AVM, Automatic Valuation Models.

The appraiser who performs an appraisal for Federally Insured Institutions must be certified or be supervised by a certified appraiser. To become an appraiser the applicant must attend classes and pass a minimal standards test. The requirements for the number of hours of education and the number of appraisals as a trainee to obtain certification changes from time to time. At present the minimum requirement for trainees is two years of apprenticeship. The appraiser must also take classes in ethics based on USPAP, which stipulate the basic appraisal methodology and guidelines. A sample of an ethics guideline for appraisers is that they must be independent and objective. Therefore an appraiser may not appraise a property that the appraiser has any interest in or anticipated interest in. Appraisers also understand that this means any family members or other close relationships. The appearance of a conflict is enough to place the value opinion and ethics of the appraiser in question.

The appraiser may not accept any additional payment or gratuity for performing an appraisal. The actual cost of the appraisal must be based on the difficulty of the appraisal and not the value of the property. Therefore, an appraiser may not state that homes up to a certain price will cost so much to appraise and homes over that amount will cost a somewhat higher price. Most appraisers will have a basic price for typical homes in an area where there are sales and consistency in models and quality, such as tract style subdivisions. Homes in a custom home area would probably be more difficult, take a longer time to complete, and require more experience, therefore a higher cost for the appraisal would be indicated. Once the fee for the appraisal is agreed upon, any offer of additional money or other item of value must not only be rejected by the appraiser but would require the appraiser to decline any further action on the appraisal and to notify the lender of the situation. The person offering the money should be aware that it could be considered a bribe in a federal transaction and could result in prosecution.

The professional appraiser, as any professional, typically would join one of the professional organizations. These organizations, such as The Appraisal Institute, have additional educational courses and seminars which offer a higher degree of knowledge about specific appraisal challenges, and also have their own governing bodies to maintain the standards and ethics of the organizations. The different designations include the MAI, SRPA, and SRA of the Appraisal Institute, the ASA designation of The American Society of Appraisers. The National Association of Realtors has created an appraisal organization with several designations. These organizations, through their different committees, police their members, and if a member were to be found guilty of violating USPAP, actions could be taken against that appraiser. The actions could be as little as an admonition, or at the opposite extreme, expulsion from the organization.

The different state boards have similar authority to admonish their appraisers who are licensed through the state. In the case of state oversight there may be similar written admonition with or without monetary penalties. The next level is typically suspension and, in extreme cases, revocation of their license. The specific finding could result in one or a combination of the above penalties. If that appraiser is found guilty of committing fraud in the appraisal, he could find himself in prison. In many cases it would be Federal prison as it would be fraud in a Federal Loan Transaction. Prison terms of up to seventeen years have been imposed in extreme cases.

In the competitive atmosphere of the lending industry, the government and secondary market have pushed for faster and less expensive methods of producing appraisals. This has resulted in a change to USPAP and now allows for several options in the appraisal process. The secondary mortgage market has for some time opted for making loans without full appraisals and uses the following choices instead of a full appraisal:

A. An Automatic Valuation Model generated by a computer
B. A drive by exterior inspection with no opinion of value
C. A drive-by appraisal without an interior inspection with an opinion of value
D. A drive-by appraisal form with an interior inspection with an opinion of value
E. A drive-by appraisal form with an interior inspection, a cost approach, and an opinion of value

There are numerous Automatic Valuation Models used and each have various levels of credibility. The best AVM's have stated that their values are only within 15% of the actual market value. This should be little comfort to the buyer who may be paying 15% more for a home than it is worth, but AVM's have been determined to satisfy the needs of the Wall Street Investors. The Investors can accept the variance in values as they purchase large numbers of loans, which they consider to balance out. In this instance only the homebuyer is hurt.

Since the AVM is not considered an appraisal by the Appraisal Foundation, an appraiser typically does not get involved, and due to the $250,000 minimum loan amount to require an appraisal, the lenders can make loans based on AVMs. The result is a value which does not typically take into account any special physical attributes of the subject or neighborhood sales. This includes condition of the subject, location of the subject, amenities of the subject or comparables, subdivision differences, such as security, or common area amenities. Some management companies now offer what they call an appraiser reviewed AVM where an appraiser, who may or may not have knowledge of the local market, reviews the sales used in the AVM and decides if the value is within reason. If the appraiser is local and has field experience in the area, this could increase the level of confidence in the AVM, but this is done in the absence of a property inspection, which may leave open the question of whether or not the improvements actually exist, and what condition the subject and comparables are in. In many areas of the country the public records do not reflect the removal of homes which have been demolished, therefore the AVM could report a value for the home which was previously on the site. This can also work the opposite way when a new home is built. The records may not have been updated resulting in the valuation of a vacant lot when in fact there are improvements which constitute most of the value of the property. To handle this concern the exterior inspection without a value could be used to make sure that the improvements exist and there are no noticeable detrimental conditions such as a highway or land fill next to the site.

The secondary mortgage market agencies have programs where, for a small processing fee, they will forego appraisals. While there are strict guidelines associated with these programs, there is no valuation or inspection of the property in the process. Based on the loan to value ratios and on the credit score of the borrower, the lenders determine what level of appraisal service is needed. In this instance there is no concern for the buyers interest in the property or for its value. If the property is in inferior condition, or in an inferior location to many homes in the area, the Automatic Valuation Model could possibly overstate the subject value. In this instance the purchaser would not know that the price paid was too high and that he made a bad deal on the property. This is where the interests of the real estate market and those of the secondary mortgage market diverge. While generally the secondary mortgage market looks for fairly priced properties in order to determine the quality of its underlying security, in the final analysis the secondary market agencies are controlled by the needs of Wall Street. Standards for underwriting pools of mortgages look at overall lending packages and are typically willing to accept minimal variances in values. This means that while a multi-million dollar package of loans has a reasonable overall value, the appraisal of a specific property within a package of loans may not have a strong correlation to the actual value of its underlying property.

The appraisal is considered to be a defensible opinion of value based on definitions of Market Value and on guidelines promulgated by government agencies. The defense of the appraisal is with the appraiser's peers in the appraisal industry and not the general public. The following Definition of Market Value is the basis of residential lending and is taken from the Statement of Limiting Conditions and Appraisers Certification on Freddie Mac Form 439 and Fannie Mae Form 1004B dated 6/93:

DEFINITION OF MARKET VALUE: The most probable price which a property should bring in a competitive and open market under all conditions requisite to a fair sale, the buyer and seller, each acting prudently, knowledgeably and assuming the price is not affected by undue stimulus. Implicit in this definition is the consummation of a sale as of a specified date and the passing of title from seller to buyer under conditions whereby: (1) buyer and seller are typically motivated; (2) both parties are well informed or well advised, and each acting in what he considers his own best interest; (3) a reasonable time is allowed for exposure in the open market; (4) payment is made in terms of cash in U.S. dollars or in terms of financial arrangements comparable thereto; and (5) the price represents the normal consideration for the property sold unaffected by special or creative financing or sales concessions granted by anyone associated with the sale.

Adjustments to the comparables must be made for special or creative financing or sales concessions. No adjustments are necessary for those costs which are normally paid by sellers as a result of tradition or law in a market area. These costs are readily identifiable since the seller pays them in virtually all-sales transactions. Special or creative financing adjustments can be made to the comparable property by comparisons to financing terms offered by a third party institutional lender that is not already involved in the property or transaction. Any adjustment should not be calculated on a mechanical dollar for dollar cost of the financing or concession, but the dollar amount of any adjustment should approximate the market's reaction to the financing or concessions based on the appraiser's judgment.

The above definition is included to point out that the appraiser is required to come to an opinion of value based on what is most probable, not what is the highest price possible. The definition also includes the fact that the buyer and seller are well informed, therefore the appraiser should not use sales of a home bought by uninformed buyers, who might be from outside the area, or who have limited knowledge of the area.

The discussion of adjustments for special terms and sales concessions is one of the most misunderstood issues by appraisers and

Realtors. Lenders do not seem to have a problem with it. For example, if furniture is included in the sale of the subject, no credit may be given for that concession. If the seller is giving a credit to the buyer at closing for closing costs or repairs, no credit can be given for that on the appraisal. Cash back at closing must be addressed if the comparables closed with this concession. As another example, a seller and buyer agree that instead of a contract for $120,000 to purchase the house, they make the contract $125,000, with a $5,000 concession. This gives the appearance of a larger down payment, while actually the buyer and seller are still dealing with $120,000. The amount the seller receives is what should be used as the final sale price after adjustments for concessions. This does not mean adjustments will be made for other costs of sale such as Realtor fees, documentary stamps, recording fees or other fees customarily paid by the seller of a property. Only the concession costs which actually reduce the legitimate sale price should be adjusted for in the appraisal.

Another major factor is that each person, seller and buyer, must be acting in their own best interest. Therefore, the appraiser must consider any known side agreements between the buyers and sellers. This protects the lender in the respect that it will have foreknowledge of a purchaser's intent to enter the transaction with less than the expected consideration, which could have a devastating impact on the overall quality of the loan transaction. The appraiser must appraise the property based on the market and not on special clauses or agreements in the contract. Still the appraiser must analyze the contract concessions and other non real estate items that might affect the contract price of the property. If the buyer and seller have a side agreement, of which the lender is unaware, they are possibly perpetrating a fraud.

The foregoing pertains mainly to residential purchase and refinance transactions. The following pertain to other users of the appraisal. In the case where the owner of a home, or the estate of the owner, requires an appraisal for the IRS, disposition of property among family members, or a divorce, the parties involved typically hire a professional CPA or lawyer to handle the affairs. If these professionals are involved in the case, they should be the one to hire the appraiser. The IRS and the courts would typically consider the appraisal to be the product of a professional. In a case where objectivity could be at issue, perhaps in disputes over estate valuations or tax claims, it is always best that any question about who hired the appraiser be answered with a statement that the work was contracted for by an individual whose interest in the final valuation is neutral. In this circumstance, when the appraiser is asked to testify, it is usually best to be able to honestly state that all discussions were with the lawyer and not with parties to the legal action. When one party or the other does the hiring in a divorce case there is typically distrust, which flows over to the people hired by the involved party. A good lawyer will not try to sway the appraiser to a specific value, as the appraiser may have to support the value on the witness stand, and a qualified appraiser hired as an expert consultant could pick apart an appraisal performed in a way to arrive at a specific value. Once valuation mistakes are pointed out in the appraisal, it may be difficult for a Judge to rely on the appraisal and frequently that appraisal and the appraiser will be disregarded.

What to expect when an appraisal is ordered

The appraiser will contact the designated access person and set up an appointment. The appraiser will react to the overall condition of the property and amenities and will take everything observable into consideration, in addition to items found out during conversations with people knowledgeable about the property.

A well maintained home, which has no obvious signs of physical problems, will appear to be worth more than a home with apparent physical problems such as peeling paint, holes in the walls, cracks in the exterior walls, water stains on the ceiling or other areas, and observable electric wires which are frayed or are not properly installed. The appraiser is usually not an engineer or a home inspector, therefore a home inspection by a qualified inspector is recommended. Items of concern which are obvious to a buyer or anyone walking through the home are noted and discussed and adjustments are made accordingly.

The homeowner should listen to his real estate sales professional about how to prepare the home for sale, and make sure that it is similarly prepared for the appraiser. When a house is freshly painted, the flooring appears well kept, the kitchen is clean and appears well maintained, and the bathrooms are mildew free and appear to be well kept, the buyer and/or the appraiser is more likely to give credit for that condition.

Once inside a home the appraiser will note the observed condition and type of the items in the home, such as the flooring, bathroom floor and wainscot, types of cabinets and counter tops, built-ins and any special wall finish. The appraiser will observe the condition of items and may actually test certain systems in the home and make any notes on items which appear to need repair or replacement. Items which affect livability are handled differently on the appraisal from items that are cosmetic in nature. Certain items affect health and safety or by code need to be replaced or repaired. Such items as broken windows, sofit screens, broken floor tiles, and holes in the walls or ceiling must be stated on the appraisal as requiring repair or replacement. Carpet cleaning, painting, cut or chipped counter tops are considered cosmetic and may affect overall condition, but do not require repair or replacement.

The furniture in the home is considered personalty and by regulation is to be given no value in the appraisal. It is always interesting when a seller tells the appraiser the price is higher than he would have accepted because the buyer purchased the furniture. Because the furniture is included in the price, the appraiser must disclose this in the appraisal. This usually results in the opinion of value being lower than the contract price. In some states, for tax reasons, it is required by law to disclose the furniture and the value placed on it.

There are many items in the home and outside of the home which may be considered personalty. The determination of this is based on the way the item is attached to the property. Items such as above ground hot tubs can be easily removed, therefore are considered personalty. In a condominium or similar type of ownership where there may be a separate deed for items like a dock or parking space. They also may not be considered as part of the real estate. In a Country Club community, where there is an equity membership in the Club, which is considered separate from the real estate, the Club membership can not be considered part of the valuation of the property. The reasoning for this is that the separately deeded equity membership, or parking space, or dock can be sold separately from the home being mortgaged. There are certain lenders who do not sell their loans in the typical secondary market and who might allow these separately deeded items to be included in the mortgage. The appraiser should then disclose that the appraisal does not meet Fannie Mae or typical secondary market guidelines.

Many buyers and sellers include an amount of the closing costs to be credited back to the buyer at closing. This is considered a sales concession. If the value of the Real Estate equals the contract price, this clause does not affect the loan. Based on secondary market guidelines there is a limit to the percentage of the sale for concessions that lenders accept. If the amount is over the percent allowed, the lender will reduce the amount of the loan. Many times when there is a concession, the seller is willing to make the concession because the sale price is higher than the market value. If the market does not reflect the higher price, the appraisal will come in lower than the sales price. If there is a side agreement not made known to the lender, the parties then become co-conspirators. This is one of the many reasons appraisers are employed by the lenders.

The appraiser hired to value a property should perform his or her own research. Depending on the local market, the appraiser may spend minutes to hours before performing the on site inspection. The appraiser should not be afraid to accept information from the parties to the transaction. He works with information received from many sources. That information is analyzed and then applied based on the appraisers' knowledge of the local market and the specific area in which the property is located. The pertinence of the information provided is based on the appraiser's interpretation of the information and its believability. If information is reported but is not verifiable, it may be considered and used as background or support for verified information.

The appraiser should request any information about the physical finish to the home. This is to check and make sure that everything has been noted and it also gives the homeowner a chance to discuss the upgrades or renovations, if any, that may or may not be readily visible. The appraiser will investigate information pertaining to any Homeowner Association, if applicable. If the property is a condominium unit, the appraiser should get the telephone number for the management company or an officer of the association to gather information about rentals, fees, including delinquent association dues, special assessments, recreational land leases and parking arrangements.

In the instance of a full appraisal report, the appraiser will measure the home. A single family home will be measured from the exterior walls, while in a condominium unit the interior dimensions are used. Any garages or car storage areas are also measured but not considered living area. The porches, patios and balconies are also measured and not included as living area. A pool or a dock attached to the site are noted and may be measured. The appraiser notes the construction type and quality of the home. The thorough appraiser will create a sketch of the interior walls of the home, indicating the bedrooms, baths, kitchen and living room. One reason for placing the actual walls is to determine if there is a normal flow to the home. Based on architectural criteria, a poor floor plan can create functional obsolescence. Examples of functional obsolescence would be if a person had to pass through a bedroom to get to another bedroom, or not having a bathroom in proximity to a bedroom whereby traffic would have to pass through other living areas to access it.

After completing the inspection of the property, the appraiser will generally inspect the comparables being used to support the appraisal report. The appraiser may have to use properties which are dissimilar in some respect to the subject property to make reasonable adjustments based on the general market perception of the value of those differences. That is to say the market or general public may pay less than or more than the cost for a certain item, once the item is in place. The appraiser must recognize the actual market value and not cost. The person spending $50,000 in upgrades should not expect the appraiser to value those upgrades dollar for dollar. The most typical example of this is a swimming pool. A pool may cost $20,000 for a basic 15 X 30 gunnite pool. In some areas of the country it may add nothing to the value of a home because of the cost of its maintenance and limited time for use, while in other areas of the country where pools are used year round, it may add $12,000 or more to the value of a home.

Normal maintenance items are not typically considered separately but are taken into account in the overall condition of the property, unless the property would not be considered livable without the maintenance item being repaired before moving into the property. Items of this kind include hot water heaters, exterior door locks, broken or missing windows, leaking roofs. These items are considered individually and may be required to be repaired by the lender before the loan can close.

The appraiser is required to confirm the sales data and conditions. This typically will require a non-public reporting service to verify the sale, as public reporting services all receive their information from the same courthouse document, which only gives a date of sale and the price paid, or a way to figure the price paid. The conditions of the sale can typically only be determined by talking to a person involved in the transaction, such as the buyer, seller or Realtor. At minimum the appraiser should confirm the sale through a Multiple Listing Service (MLS) or other private reporting service if available. Otherwise the appraiser should try to contact the seller or buyer. If none of this is possible, the appraiser should not use the sale, or if the sale appears reasonable and within the typical market, a disclosure as to the extent of verification should be made. This should rarely happen in most urban or suburban areas as there should be enough sales to use which can be confirmed through other than public record sources. If verification is not possible, and if the sale is used, it should be given less weight in the final analysis.

In the case of a subject home having a pool, the appraiser would look for other homes with a pool. This would negate any need to adjust for this major item. The appraiser will also look for homes in similar condition to the subject and with similar finish as this would result in a higher level of confidence in the opinion of value. The appraiser will then look at all the differences between the subject and comparables and decide which comparable is most similar to the subject and weight that sale the most in the final reconciliation. The weight placed on that sale might be tempered by the date of the sale and terms of the sale in relationship to the dates of sale and terms of the sale for the other comparables.

The following list is a summary of what an appraiser looks at when comparing the subject to the comparables. The list is not exhaustive but gives a basic idea of why the appraiser uses certain sales and not others.

General Description of the Improvements:
    1. Are they similar to other improvements in area.
    2. Age of the subject similar to homes in the market area
    3. The material used and quality of the improvement.
    4. Is size similar to size of homes in the market area
    5. Are amenities similar to homes in the market area

Site Information
    1. Is site size typical of the subdivision or market area
    2. Is the site functional - can the whole site be used
    3. Is the site location different from most homes in area
    4. Is the site location similar to the comparables location
    5. Is the site view described definitively

Neighborhood Description:
    1. Is the neighborhood accurately defined
    2. Are the boundaries reasonable
    3. Are the homes similar to each other
    4. Is the subject in a defined subdivision or in a PUD or large complex with amenities

Comparables Analysis:
    1. Are the sales in the same project or a section of the same project
    2. Are the comparables similar in size and utility
    3. Do condos have the same room count
    4. Do comparables have same quality of finish to the subject, such as roofing and siding
    5. Do the comparables have a similar view to the subject
    6. Are the lot sizes similar
    7. Are the comparables a similar age or are they newer or older

8. Are the amenities similar
9. Are sales verified through sources other than Public Record
10. Are non-realty items included

Common Conceptions and Misconceptions

There are sometimes misconceptions about the guidelines as stated by Fannie Mae. An example of this is that in condominiums there must be two sales from within the development and one sale from outside. This was included by Fannie Mae under its new construction guidelines, so as not to have a builder set his own market. If there are enough re-sales to determine a market in the subject condominium project, and the project is of sufficient size, the appraiser is at liberty to stay within the project if by doing so that will create a more accurate value conclusion. However, if the project has a minimal number of units and there are similar small projects nearby, it may make sense to go outside of the project. The same is true for subdivisions. If the development is new with only one builder, then the guideline requires one sale from within, one sale from outside the development and one sale at the appraiser's discretion. In older projects with re-sales, the appraiser should try to stay inside the development. The guideline states that the best sales are from within the same subdivision or condominium. If the lender has a legitimate reason for requiring an outside sale, the appraiser should be made aware of this and then it is up to the appraiser to determine if the request is reasonable and legitimate.

Another guideline that is frequently misunderstood is that sales in an urban or suburban market must be within a mile. If a comparable property is used that is across a major barrier such as a highway or river, that would separate the market characteristics for one property from the subject property, then stating that a property is comparable because it is within that one mile limit would be faulty reporting. Using comparables more than a mile away but with the same market characteristics would be more appropriate in such instances. Staying within the subdivision does not guarantee a good appraisal as there can be many differences between homes even in the same neighborhood. As an example, a home on a dry lot could be compared to the house across the street which happens to be on a waterfront lot. In such a situation adjustments must be noted in order to bring in a value conclusion of quality.

As with every profession and job, there are circumstances which happen and only through experience will the appraiser know how to handle non-typical situations. It is a USPAP requirement that an appraiser be competent and qualified to handle the property to be appraised. If the appraiser is not competent and qualified, then the appraiser may tell the client that he will align himself with another appraiser experienced in that type of property and they would both perform the appraisal.

Building/Home Inspections
by
Bruce Sage

In the mid 1980's and early 1990's lenders determined that one of the many contributing causes of failed mortgages was the catastrophic expenses associated with roof failures and structural damage to wood members caused by termite infestation. To react to this increase in the foreclosure rates, as well as pressure from federal regulators, they quietly adopted a policy of requiring loan applicants to obtain a roof condition inspection and a termite inspection (Report of Wood Destroying Organisms) prior to releasing the funding package.

General, building and residential contractors, roofing contractors and carpenters, along with a cast of non-licensed entrepreneurs, made a business of cold calling on Real Estate Brokers to solicit opportunities from their associates to perform these roof inspections. At the same time, legitimate pest control companies replicated the process with respect to performing termite inspections.

As this practice took approximately two years to become a universal or household word among the lending community, some creative thinkers began to add to the requirement Radon Gas and Lead Based Paint inspections. In 1988 the United States Environmental Protection Agency published a standard for the maximum acceptable level of Radon Gas of 4.0 pCi/L (pico curies per liter), along with a three-tiered zone mapping system. By this time everyone and his brother had jumped on the bandwagon and required it. Finally, after many years of exhaustive testing and many millions of dollars spent by consumers, the industry learned that certain geographic areas are not prone to the formation of Radon gas pockets in the soil and these areas were eventually made exempt by most lenders. In many states the majority of property was found to be well under the 4.0pCi/L standard. Homes and buildings where the levels were found to be above the 4.0 pCi/L were required to be posted with an appropriate warning notice informing the occupants and public of a potential health hazard. A better understanding of this mapping and grading system can be found on the Internet at: www. epa.gov/iaq/radon/zonemap.html.

Lead based paint was taken off the market in 1978, thus any home constructed prior to this date was, and still is, a potential target for testing.

The overall response to these new requirements literally caused doctors, lawyers, accountants, contractors and others who saw these requirements as personal financial opportunities to open inspection businesses dedicated to the testing for Radon Gas and Lead Based Paint. And for many years, this became a cash cow.

In more recent times lenders are far more conservative and educated with respect to Radon Gas and Lead Based Paint. However, in an abundance of caution, and in order to protect itself from litigation, the Real Estate industry tends to continue issuing disclosure information regarding these two hazards.

Since many homes located in the south, southwest, southeast and west are engineered with very pricey cement tile, wood shake and other cement type roofing products, replacement of these design elements shortly after taking possession would likely impose a severe financial hardship to the owner.

Termite infestations can range from very minor to severe depending upon the species of termites, the length of time the colony has had to occupy, multiply and eat away at structural elements such as truss members, studs, rafters, sheathing and other wood members. Depending upon the geographic location, some species can even work their way through concrete (Florida-Formosan Termite). These tenacious insects were brought to the United States on container ships from the Far East. They excrete an acid which burns holes in concrete products, thus enabling the colony to progress vertically through a building.

Termites are generally most active during what is called the 'swarm season'. This varies according to the geographic area and climatic conditions. The more wood utilized in the construction, the greater a problem there is with structural failures caused by termites. In areas experiencing this problem there has been a shift in home design from the "California" designs with exceptionally large amounts of wood, to more contemporary designs which utilize plastics and stucco to simulate the that look. Since wood is the mainstay of the termites' diet, the less wood used for structural components, the lower potential for catastrophic damage as a result of termite infestations.

In addition to the termite, most state statutes consider "woodrot fungus" a form of wood destroying organism. Simply put, this is a mold that forms on wood as a result of excessive exposure to water. This fungus eats the wood as part of its food supply. The most common areas are the fascia, soffits, truss members, roof and wall sheathing, doors and doorjambs and decorative trim. While much of woodrot fungus results from poor maintenance of roofs and exterior wood treatment, the reality is that this problem will be with us for as long as we continue to use wood as a building product. With the introduction of metals and plastics into the housing market, many of these construction elements are being replaced.

Roof sheathing and trusses are usually well protected until the roof covering is compromised either by age, weather or both. In tropical climates, roof coverings do not last as long as they would in more moderate climates. In areas where severe winters with large amount of snow are typical, the escaping heat from the attic space melts the snow from under the surface and, with the right temperatures, causes water to accumulate between the roofing and the underlayment.

Soon, the underlayment fails and water intrudes into the attic space. The end result is woodrot fungus. Since this fungus is progressive, it destroys the structural integrity of the wood product and can compromise the integrity of the building.

Regulation

Most states have been reluctant to take ownership of regulation with respect to the inspector who conducts the roof inspection. As an example, Florida does not regulate such inspectors. In an attempt to shrink government and thus regulation, Florida has encouraged privatization. Home Inspectors can belong to a private association that claims to be "self-policing." The reason the states shy away from regulation is that it puts a financial burden on them and imposes a manpower requirement on already thinly stretched resources. Thus, the original roof inspection business has expanded into a full blown home or building inspection business. Regulation of such a business would cover at a minimum structural, electrical, plumbing and mechanical trades normally associated with new construction currently regulated under various municipal authorities. The sole exception to this, the Termite Inspector, is regulated under various laws because he operates for a legitimate pest control company.

Many States such as Alabama have taken a giant step forward and created a licensing process for "Home Inspectors." The states that have followed this path are now collecting data and sharing it with those who do not license this trade to determine if state control of the licensing has any impact on consumer fraud and quality control. At the same time, many of those previously alluded to private associations have hired expensive lobbyists to battle against regulation to insure their survival. To date, most self-regulating industries have not lived up to their mission statements and the consumer continues to suffer on account of it. Most states do however, regulate Radon Gas Inspectors as well as the laboratories that process the samples and report the results.

Complete Home/Building Inspections

Today, almost every transaction involving residential, commercial and industrial buildings involves an inspection. While the lending community continues to focus mainly on the "Roof and Termite" aspect, the prospective buyer and buyer's agent purchase complete or comprehensive inspections. The difference between the "Roof and Termite" inspection and the "Comprehensive Inspections" is significant. The comprehensive inspection includes the "Roof and Termite" inspections, and adds electrical, plumbing, appliances, air-conditioning, windows and doors, building structure, foundation, swimming pool and equipment, and irrigation and equipment. While the lending community focuses on only two items as having the potential for catastrophic expense and thus mortgage failure, replacement of air-conditioning equipment, major appliances and swimming pools and related equipment, can easily equal or exceed the financial impact of a roof failure or termite damage. Pools have been known to crack due to structural failures. Others have been pushed out of the ground due to underground streams or unusually high water tables. At some time or other most require the final surface called Marcite or Diamondbright™ to be resurfaced.

The key term relating to an inspection is 'functional'. The inspector is not going to rate a roof, air-conditioner or any other part of the home on a scale of one to ten with respect to how well it works. He/she should only be concerned about what it is doing at the time of the inspection and not how efficiently it is performing. To over-simplify, it is either working or not. The roof is either free from leaks and in satisfactory condition or not.

147

Life Expectancy

Life expectancy is purely an estimate based on reported data dependent upon geographic location, care, use, maintenance, home environment and weather conditions. Some of these estimates will vary. Further it should be noted that as with any mechanical or manufactured item, premature failures can and do occur. To assist both the purchaser and or the lender in understanding frequency of replacement, below is a list of items and the general life expectancy which their respective industry has experienced.

Roofs:

1. Asphalt Shingles: 15-20 years (North), 12-15 years (South & Southwest)
2. Asphalt Multi-Thickness Shingles: 20-25 years (North), 15-18 years (South & Southwest)
3. Asphalt/Fiberglass Shingles: 5-20 years (North), 12-15 years (South & Southwest)
4. Asphalt Roll Roofing: 8-12 years (North), 6-10 years (South & Southwest)
5. Built-up Roofing: 15-20 years (North), 8-12 years (South & Southwest)
6. Wood Shingles/Shakes: 15-30 years (North), 10-15 years (South & Southwest)
7. Clay or Concrete Tiles: 20-25 years
8. Slate Shingles: 20-100 years
9. Metal Roofing: 15-40+ years
10. Single-Ply Membranes: 15-25 years

Major Appliances

1. Dishwasher: 5-10 years
2. Garbage Disposal: 3-5 years

3. Ranges/Ovens: 10-15 years
4. Refrigerator: 10-15 years
5. Exhaust Fan: 15-20 years
6. Clothes Washer: 5-8 years
7. Clothes Dryer: 5-10 years
8. Instant Hot Water Dispensers: 2-4 years
9. Air-conditioners 12-17 years (depending upon climate)
10. Microwave Ovens 5-10 years

Swimming Pool & Spa Equipment

Swimming pool and spa pumps, motor and impeller seal replacement: 2-3 years

1. Pool & Spa Filters: 8-15 years
2. Solar Pool & Spa Heating Panels: 5-10 years
3. Solar Pool & Spa Heating Controls & Automatic Valves: 3-8 years
4. Natural & LP Gas Pool and Spa Heaters: 6-10 years
5. Electric Spa Heaters: 5-8 years
6. Electric Pool & Spa Heat Pumps: 6-10 years
7. Swimming Pool & Spa Light Transformer: 8-15 years

Plumbing Equipment

1. Hot water heaters: 10 years (depending upon mineral content of water)
2. Bathtub: Life of building
3. Cast Iron, Stainless Steel & China Sinks: Life of building
4. Porcelain On Steel Sinks: 5-10 years (depending upon water conditions)
5. Toilets: Life of building (with maintenance)
6. Faucets: 8-14 years (depending upon water conditions)

7. Shower Pans (new PVC & molded acrylic) 20-30 years
8. Shower Pans (galvanized) 10-14 years

Structural Items

Windows: life of building (with maintenance)

1. Steel Garage Doors: 15-25 years
2. Wood Garage Doors: 10-15 years (depending upon weather and maintenance)
3. Electric Garage Door Openers: 5-10 years (with maintenance)
4. Wood Entrance Doors: 8-12 years (depending upon climate and protection from weather)
5. Metal Clad Entrance Doors: 10-18 years (depending upon climate and protection from weather)

Irrigation Equipment

Irrigation Pump Motors: 5 years

1. Hydro Indexing Valves: 5 years (with maintenance and depending upon water source)
2. Solenoid Valves: 3-10 years

One must keep in mind that this is only a barometer and not a statement that because an air-conditioner is twenty years old, it will have to be replaced. Only the inspector can determine its current condition. Temperature comparisons, equipment physical condition, air flow, and duct conditions are only some of the indicators the experienced inspector uses to determine if it is functional.

Can the Seller Refute the Results of an Inspection?

In most states, the seller has the right to bring his/her own inspector into the picture. When this is done, both the purchaser's and sellers agents will compare the results and report them to their respective clients. If, at this point the purchaser and seller cannot agree on the results, they can be given the opportunity to select a third inspector whose results are not refutable. Contract law provides for who pays for the second and third inspections.

Who Makes the Repairs?

The contract for purchase dictates the party responsible for paying for repairs as well as the maximum percentage of the purchase price that party will be obligated to pay. But more and more contracts for real estate purchase are being written 'as is' with the right of inspection, meaning that the purchaser has the right to back out of the deal based upon the results of the inspection. When repairs are made, most contracts clearly specify that the work must be performed by a licensed tradesman. This is one of the most often misunderstood terms in the contract. It could be interpreted in such a way that if electrical and structural repairs were needed, that the licensed electrician would do his part and the work of other tradesmen too. Further, many states, and local governments have stopped issuing licenses for the "handyman." While handymen still perform home repairs, they are rarely asked to produce a license. The handyman's prices might be cheaper, but he/she may not be doing the work properly. Unless the work is re-inspected, the purchaser may inherit a potential disaster.

Replacement of Damages Caused by Termites

This is an area that literally comes back to bite the buyer. However insignificant the damage may be to a truss member or piece of wood trim, it is likely that after the Termite Treatment (chemical or gas) is completed, and unless the damaged lumber is replaced, the next Termite Inspection Report performed when the property is sold again will identify that area as still having evidence of termite infestation. As a standard practice, the inspection company will recommend another treatment. This is done to avoid liability. Many lenders will not release funding unless there is a clear report evidencing no live infestation. For example, it is possible that damage from a ten year old treatment was never repaired, yet the home was tented and the house changed hands twice before it became an issue with the most recent lender. The best advise one can give to both lenders and purchasers is to not accept anything less than removal of damaged lumber after a treatment. Only the trained structural inspector can determine if the structural integrity of lumber has been compromised.

Should there be a Reinspection?

Without having a re-inspection performed, how else does the purchaser know the work was done correctly? The re-inspection is an investment in prevention. Often deficiencies can be traced back to the inspection that was performed when the sellers purchased the home, and no re-inspection was performed to protect them.

Goals of the Home/Building Inspection

In order to provide the consumer with a value added service, the home/building inspection should include but not be limited to a thorough functional test and or visual inspection of all of the elements of the home or building without causing damage or impeding the future function of its many elements. Use of rating scales such as poor, fair, good and excellent or numeric values is misleading to the client.

1. Determine if the equipment or element is functional.
2. Report, on an objective basis only, the current status of all items tested or observed.
3. Identify any item not functional.
4. Identify any item which cannot be accessed for inspection and cause.

5. Provide an easy to read report, using language which does not require an engineering degree to understand.
6. Provide estimates based upon current geographic market prices or licensed tradesmen in each discipline to correct the deficiency
7. Avoid making any predictions with respect to longevity as there are too many variables which could prove the inspector inaccurate, such as weather patterns, abuse and neglect by the user to name a few.

The reporting process must, under all conditions, be objective vs. subjective. Inspection reports must clearly avoid the use of terms that reflect the personal opinion of the inspector, and it is unethical for the home inspector to offer to make any repairs based upon his own inspection results. Inspectors' fees should be affordable and they should make themselves accessible after the inspection has been completed for clarification of questions pertaining to the inspected property. The consumer should be careful to read any disclaimer statement that he/she is asked to sign prior to the conduct of the inspection. Failure to understand such a document can compromise their legal rights in the event the inspection company makes serious mistakes during the inspection or in the preparation of the report.

For more information visit: http://www.floridamoldsrus.com

What Everyone Should Know about Mold
by
Bruce Sage

According to historians, microbiologists and the medical community, fungi, mold and mold spores preceded pre-historic man. It has been determined that the presence of mold is a key element in the balance of nature, because mold causes the breakdown or decay of dead plant material. Mold is the largest biomass on earth. Without it our predecessors would have been buried alive under refuse of dead, but not decayed, plant material. As such, no fungus or mold ever evolved to live indoors.

Molds have been studied for years and the ongoing studies have produced startling information as to how they survive indoors, the medical impact they have on humans, and the destructive forces they posses with respect to common materials used in the construction of our homes, office buildings and schools.

As a result of recent collaborative research between the EPA (Environmental Protection Agency), CDC (Center for Disease Control) and private research institutions, along with frequently published and televised specials strictly devoted to mold, society has been made to live in fear of the "M" word. Further, the news media has focused on some very high profile court cases involving the failure of insurance carriers to act diligently with respect to mold damage claims, as well as documented mold-related child deaths in the State of Ohio and large numbers of faculty, staff and students reporting a wide range of unusual illnesses resulting from contamination of the schools they work in or attend in several states.(visit: http://www.epa.gov/).

Mold is now a major concern for the employer, employee, parents, home buyer, home seller, Realtor, lender and insurer.

Technical Aspects

Molds are classified into three distinct categories with respect to how they impact the health of humans: allergenic, pathogenic, Mycotoxic

Of course, the third item is the one that gets most of the publicity in the form of phrases like "Black Mold". While there are some 72,000 species of molds, this one stands out because of the data which the E.P.A. and C.D.C. have published. While the media has given major emphasis to this particular classification and specifically a mold species called Stachybotrys, an individual who has a reduced or compromised immune system could react to a mold classified as allergenic with symptoms equally as severe as another would react to a mold which is myotoxigenic.

There are many medical reasons that explain why different people react to the same mold differently, but in general, it is the wide variance in personal immune systems to defend themselves against these agents that explains why two people living in the same home react with totally different symptoms.

Molds need only three simple environmental conditions to collect, and reproduce: moisture, food source and an amiable temperature. Moisture appears to be the most difficult component to control. The geographic region under consideration determines how difficult a task it is to keep moisture at or below the 50% relative humidity level suggested by the E.P.A. For example, states like Arizona, Nevada and New Mexico are typically very dry and at the same time hot during the summer months. In order to keep people comfortable during those months, moisture is added to the air by using equipment like "Swamp Coolers" or "Moisture Injection Systems". On the other hand, in Florida, a tropical climate, maintaining a 50% or lower relative humidity level requires either an air cooled or water cooled air-conditioning system which must be running at peak efficiency during the majority of the year. In some climates a simple de-humidifier is utilized to maintain the indoor climate within acceptable limits. It is not uncommon for people who own more than one home to close the one they are not occupying and fail to maintain the 50% or less humidity level. Further, some of those who close their properties forget to turn the main water valve off as part of the closing procedure. In addition, poor maintenance is blamed as a major contributing factor for the inability to control moisture regardless of the region. Such things as leaking water valves, faucets, water closets, shower pans, roof leaks and air-conditioner condensate pans are just a few additional contributing factors added to the task of maintaining humidity.

One of the most important parts of maintenance is a semi-annual air-conditioner service. This determines the condition of the coils, freon levels and overall system performance. Monthly changing of filters is very important to efficient system operation. Failure to change the filter will cause the system to work harder to achieve the desired temperature and relative humidity. Further, when the filter is dirty, less air flows over the cold coils and the end result is, at a minimum, excessive cooling of less air with a greater chance that the coil will freeze. Even when the coil does not freeze, the system collects about twice the volume of moisture. The pan, which is responsible for collecting and ultimately passing the condensate to the drain, cannot handle the volume. In this case, either the pan overflows into the intake plenum or the system blower sucks the excessive moisture back into the air it is distributing to the ducts. The later can cause mold formation within the ducts and or the home. Repeated freezing of a coil can render the system inoperable.

Next is the food source. Most molds thrive on cellulose products. It is difficult to appreciate the amount of cellulose that is found in construction and home decoration products. For example here are just a few: (1) sheet rock; (2) lumber; (3) paint; (4) wallpaper; (5) wallpaper adhesive; (6) drapes and fabrics; (7) insulation. Since these cannot simply be eliminated from building interiors the better choice is to prevent them from accessing moisture.

Temperature is vital to the growth of molds. Generally speaking, some exceptions granted, the higher the temperature, the higher the humidity. It is the things that are done to lower the temperature that can impact the ability to grow mold, and building design plays an important part in this. High ceiling designs with poor ventilation in the upper portion of the ceiling causes the higher elevation to be much hotter and more humid. Further, Architects and Mechanical Engineers for years designed air-conditioning distribution systems that placed the cool air below the highest elevation and thus created a natural point of condensation. As the heat rises, it passes through the cooler layers of air and forms moist hot air which remains at the higher elevations. The cathedral ceiling is a good example of this concept. It is not uncommon to find mold colonies growing at the higher elevation on wood and sheet rock finished ceilings.

The challenge is to maintain an indoor environment that is dry and cool but not cold, so that mold spores, which enter the home from the exterior as a result of doors or windows being opened, cannot thrive indoors. Additional information on how to control the indoor environment can be found on the EPA website. Publications of the EPA can be printed from that site.

How Do Humans Become Contaminated?

Humans generally become contaminated because their indoor environment has an amplified mold spore count. They can ingest spores through the food they eat, absorb spores through their skin and inhale spores through the nose and mouth.

Common health effects of mold are:

1. Allergic Reaction: the most common, inhalation or touching of spores
2. Asthma: mold spores can trigger or make asthma worse

3. Hypersensitivity Pneumonitis: develop after acute or chronic exposure
4. Irritants: contamination of the eyes, mouth, throat etc.
5. Opportunistic Infections: invasion into an immuno-compromised host
6. Mycotoxic: fungal poisons, only limited data for humans
7. Glucans: Organic Dust Toxic Syndrome (ODTS), flu-like symptoms

Impact on Buildings and Insurance Carriers

As profound as the impact mold has on human health, it has also proven to be a destructive force on buildings. In the lending, insurance and inspection business the term "Woodrot Fungus" is used. This is a classic example of the destructive force nature can have on buildings. Mold, given plenty of moisture, and limited access to sunlight, will eat through structural members such as studs, trusses, firing strips, doors and door jambs, sheet rock and many other building products. More and more eyes are turning to mold as a villain with respect to not only health issues, but also potentially expensive and almost catastrophic repair costs. In most cases, owner neglect has been proven to blame for insurance claims related to mold. As a result, insurance underwriters have applied to and obtained various exposure reductions (depending upon the state). It is important to keep in mind that the insurance companies can write into their policies time limits or statutes of limitations on claims of this nature. In other words, if the adjuster can prove that the cause existed beyond the limitation stated in the policy, then the claim can be denied. Further, the insurer is only responsible for the repairs of the damage caused, less the deductible, but not for the cause. Some states have granted insurers the right to totally exclude mold damage coverage or offer the homeowner the option to purchase a mold rider or additional coverage above and beyond the maximum allowed in their policy.

With this in mind, the best advice is to bring in a professional mold testing company and a certified mold remediation company to obtain estimates of the repairs and file an insurance claim immediately. If the insurance company does not respond quickly, it is suggested that the property owner document the damage with photographs and perform the minimum necessary remediation procedures to protect both the health of the occupants and the structural integrity of the home or building. Most insurance policies have provisions that address emergencies and procedures to be followed.

Mold Impact on Lenders

It is too early to determine the exact impact mold in homes and buildings will have on the loan process. Awareness of mold and related issues is currently under study by the lending industry. It is very likely that procedures will be implemented that take mold inspections into consideration much like the roof and termite inspections already in force.

Mold Impact on Realtors

While the lending industry is lagging behind in its data collection and the possibility for additional financial burden on the purchaser or seller of a property, many city and county boards of Realtors have already had their legal advisors write new language into listing and sales contracts offering mold inspections to potential purchasers, but not mandating it. In addition, they are requiring sellers to make disclosure statements with respect to mold events. This is being done to minimize post sale legal exposure.

Mold Is Not A Deal Killer

Mold in a home or building is no more a deal killer than woodrot fungus or termites. Unfortunately, the media can and does pick up and publish stories that make people paranoid. The burning down or bulldozing of homes and buildings is a very extreme and isolated method of resolving a problem that most likely could have been addressed far more conservatively if not neglected. It can be addressed by specialists who are specially trained in the location, removal and repair of construction materials once contaminated with mold. The Certified Remediator is usually a licensed general, building, or residential contractor who has received training on how to find the source of water, protect the balance of the property from cross-contamination during removal, remove and replace damaged construction materials and restore the home or building to a pre-mold condition. The earlier the Remediation Contractor is brought into the picture, the lower the cost of remediation. Once the work is completed, the home or building is retested and certified not to have an amplified spore count. With the exception of natural disasters such as floods and hurricanes, remediation will usually cost less than $10,000, provided remediation commences early enough.

Mold Inspectors

There are no federal regulations or guidelines pertaining to residential mold inspections. Individuals who conduct such inspections receive their training from either legitimate laboratories certified by the E.P.A. or other credible environmental quality associations, or they can obtain it from privately held seminars. In the absence of federal intervention, most states are reluctant to tackle the problem of inspector training, licensing and regulation. The exception is the City of New York where the Department of Health has published "Guidelines on Assessment and Remediation of Fungi in Indoor Environments". While this is a set of guidelines that does not imply regulation, it does show that the city is being proactive and regulation will most likely be forthcoming.

As is the case with anything as new as mold assessment or testing, the more training the inspector has and the more time on the job lends to his credibility. Such things as the inspection technique, equipment calibration, records, extensive interviews with the property owner to understand the history of the property to be inspected, experience in the construction industry and any licenses held related to building inspections contribute to a fair and informative inspection.

Environmental Assessment

A visual inspection must be conducted of the entire property in question. An inspector should not resort to scare tactics before, during or after the inspection. His job is purely to collect sufficient data from the occupant(s) to facilitate his visual inspection. The inspector should create a checklist so that he has a standardized list of questions that will aid him in doing a thorough job. The inspector must focus on such things as the ventilation system and items high in cellulose content such as sheetrock, ceiling tiles or wallpaper. The use of a moisture meter would assist him in locating areas where the moisture level is unusually higher than comparable locations. Depending upon the type of equipment used, moisture located in hidden areas can be detected. The inspector must understand all systems and look for:

1. Possible leaks, damage to truss members along with insulation and the upper side of the ceiling material.
2. Cracks in exterior walls as well as those which are replicated on the interior.
3. Water stains on walls, ceilings, window and door jambs are good indicators of water incursion.
4. Obvious repairs around water supply pipes, drains and shower pans. Leaking traps, stains on bathroom vanities and kitchen sink cabinets.
5. Stains in closets where air-conditioning equipment is installed.
6. The inspector should look at any penetrations between the

outside and inside of a wall as a potential source of water incursion.

7. Cracks and or loose tiles in showers must be noted.
8. Temperature and humidity tests should be conducted to determine if the air-conditioning equipment is capable of extracting moisture from the air and removing it through the condensate line without restriction.
9. The duct system should be checked for leaks.
10. The seal between the air-handler and the plenum must be free from leaks. Musty odors generally are a clue that there has been a water incursion or spill.
11. Carpets and padding should be checked along with the tackless strips along the outside walls and walls adjacent to bathrooms for discoloration or water stains.
12. Cabinet bases should be checked for swelling due to water absorption.
13. The air handler coil should be checked for excessive dirt accumulation and mold growth.

Sampling Inspection

In view of the fact that there are many different types of equipment and laboratories, it would be unfair to dictate a particular sampling procedure. It is however important to sample visible mold in each room. If air samples are to be taken, it is strongly recommended that one sample be taken for each air-conditioning zone and one for each floor in residential buildings. Further, it is very important to take at least one air sample from the exterior as a comparison. With larger homes, mold spores can become trapped in areas that, by virtue of their design, block the spores from mixing with those that are present in other or nearby areas. Therefore additional sampling is indicated and should be performed. This is a judgment the experienced inspector must make. Each laboratory and equipment manufacturer will provide its inspectors with recommendations on the use of their products.

Regardless of the amount and type of sampling the inspector chooses, it is important to understand that sampling represents a picture in time. The indoor environment is not static, rather it changes based upon the lifestyle of the occupants. Frequent opening of doors and windows can increase the spore count as spores from the exterior enter freely. On exceptionally humid days, the mold spores stay closer to the ground and move around with a little wind. Leaving doors or windows open will allow these spores to enter the home.

An important part of testing protocol is that the testing equipment must be calibrated at each job site. Further, air samples should not be drawn from the exterior if it is raining. Inclement weather can distort the results of the inspectors control sample.

The Inspection Report

While the inspection report must contain a significant amount of technical information to aid in the remediation process, it should be written in a way that the consumer can understand. The purpose of the report is not to put fear into the property owner, but to direct him to a resolution of the problem. Providing the client with reference materials or access to government publications is very helpful. When remediation is indicated, then it should be recommended. The inspector should remain neutral at all times and, because of the appearance of impropriety in performing both functions, the inspector and remediator should not be the same person. Post remediation inspections should be conducted to certify that the remediation was successful. If the Mold Inspector wants to make recommendations with respect to Remediation Contractors, he should give several names from which to choose.

The Role of the Physician

Since mold has only recently been identified as a potentially harmful agent with respect to human health, the role of the physician is now changing. For years Allergists and Ear, Nose and Throat Specialists have routinely conducted allergy testing and desensitization to develop a stronger human immune response to allergens. However, with the new knowledge being made available to the physician, he is taking a much more in depth approach to treatment. Questions are being asked about the home and or work environment to determine what contributing factors may play into the symptoms the patient is presenting. Many physicians are recommending mold testing of the home and workplace to enable them to either rule out or include in the program of treatment. Mold Inspectors are not medical professionals and as such can only provide the results of testing to aid the physicians in their attempt to solve what may be a set of complex problems. Many physicians provide their patients with a survey form complete. These forms enable patients to catalogue either their homes or workplaces with specific answers to the content, lifestyles and how the time of day symptoms present relate either the home or work place. The same applies to children attending school. In many cases, it takes communication between the primary care physician and the specialists. Usually this is seen in the form of exchange of medical records. As more information becomes available from the E.P.A. and the C.D.C., physicians, inspectors and remediators can work in harmony toward a common goal. . . the health and welfare of human beings.

For more information visit: www.moldsrus.com

Glossary of Mold Related Terms

1. **Fungi:** any of a major group (Fungi) of saprophytic and parasitic spore-producing organisms usually classified as plants that lack chlorophyll and include molds, rusts, mildews, smuts, mushrooms, and yeasts*

2. **Spores:** primitive, usually unicellular, often environmentally resistant, dormant or reproductive body produced by plants and some microrganisms and capable of development into a new individual either directly or after fusion with another spore *

3. **Cellulose:** a polysaccharide (C6H10O5)x of glucose units that constitutes the chief part of the cell walls of plants; occurs naturally in such fibrous products as cotton and kapok, and is the raw material of many manufactured goods (as paper, rayon, and cellophane) *

4. **Biomass:** the amount of living matter (as in a unit area or volume of habitat) *

5. **Allergen:** a substance that induces allergy *

6. **Pathogen:** causing or capable of causing disease *

7. **Mycotoxin:** a toxic substance produced by a fungus and especially a mold *

8. **C.D.C.:** The United States Centers for Disease Control

9. **E.P.A.:** The United States Environmental Protection Agency

10. **Plenum:** A duct connection to either the air intake or air supply side of the air handler

11. **Freon:** A gas that is used in air-conditioning equipment often referred to as refrigerant

*http://www.merriamwebster.com

Part V

Insurance Clearly Understood

Title Insurance
by
Peter M. Lopez, Esq.

What is title insurance? What does it cover? Who is protected by it? These are all questions most people have as they begin the process of buying a home and they review their Good Faith Estimate. It is important for borrowers and lenders to understand the types of title insurance, who and what is covered under a typical policy, and how coverage under a typical policy can be modified and expanded.

Title insurance, like most other forms of insurance, is a contract between two parties, the title insurance company and the insured. The coverage is defined by the terms and conditions of the title insurance policy and the exceptions from coverage listed therein. Therefore, it is important for homebuyers and lenders to read and understand the title insurance commitment and final title policy in order that they might understand who and what is covered, and what is excluded from the terms of the policy.

But why is title insurance needed and how did it develop? The beginnings of the title insurance industry arose out of the need for adequate assurances as to the method of conveying real property. When a person purchases a parcel of real property, how does he know if he is dealing with the true owner. Prior to title insurance, an examiner would search the public records and determine who the proper owner was and whether their title was subject to any liens or encumbrances. An opinion of title was prepared and relied upon by the lender and the owner. Therefore, the parties relied on the expertise of the examiner and on the examiner's reputation in dealing with the condition of the title.

As time went on, and as the population grew, it became clear that a person's title was only as good as the examiner's knowledge and experience. The courts also were reluctant to hold examiners responsible for unanticipated defects in title. When "hidden" defects arose, the purchasers were left without any recourse. Moreover, the secondary market, where mortgages are bought and sold, required some type of financial backing in the event a defect in the title was discovered after the origination of a new mortgage. Thus, title insurance was created in order to have an efficient mechanism in place to deal with claims on title for the secondary market and to allow a buyer some recourse, through an insurance company's financial backing, in the event a valid claim was made on title to a property. Title insurance provides buyers and lenders with an option to cover the risk associated with unanticipated defects in title. There are two types of title insurance policies: an owner's policy and a lender's policy. The main difference between these types of policies is the entity and the instrument being insured.

The owner's policy will insure a grantee of a Warranty Deed, that is, the new owner of a parcel of property. The owner's policy provides coverage for as long as the named insured has an interest in the property and is typically issued for the amount of the purchase price. The buyer's title to the property will be defended by the title insurance company in the event a defect in title is discovered or a claim is made against the buyer's title. Before issuing a title insurance policy, the title insurance company or its agent will search the public records to determine whether any instruments are recorded against the title to the subject property. The search is completed to determine ownership of the property and to identify any liens that encumber title to the property.

A lender's policy, on the other hand, will insure the grantee of a mortgage. The lender's policy is issued in the amount of the loan and only provides coverage for the life of the loan. Once the loan is paid in full and satisfied, the loan policy is no longer in effect and the lender is not afforded any protection under the lender policy. However, if a claim is made that the "owner" is not the lawful owner of the property, the lender's policy will defend the lender from any losses that the lender may incur. Lender's policies also are a declining balance insurance policy, in that, as the loan is paid over time and the principal balance is reduced, the coverage afforded under the policy is likewise reduced.

A title insurance company will conduct a search of the public records to determine the lawful owner of the property and whether anyone else has an interest in the property. However, even a thorough search cannot discover certain "hidden" defects to title that can only be efficiently protected by title insurance. These "hidden" defects are the basis for many claims.

The first of these "hidden" defects is forgery. In the event a person signs a deed claiming to be the owner of the property, the buyer is not protected without title insurance. The forgery could occur in the subject transaction or in the previous chain of title. How does a buyer know that the seller is who he says he is? It is difficult for any buyer to protect himself from this risk. However, most title policies will protect the buyer and the lender from this type of "hidden" defect.

Undisclosed heirs are another form of hidden defect. When a person owning real property dies, his interest in the property passes to his heirs. One of the heirs is generally named as the personal representative of the estate of the deceased and that person is responsible for administering the assets of the estate and conveying them to the proper heirs. On occasion, an heir is unknowingly left out of the process and may return long after the real estate has been sold to a third party. The omitted heir's interest in the property is superior to the new property owner, even though the new owner has purchased the property. Without title insurance, the new owner would have to defend a lawsuit filed by the omitted heir and the new owner would likely lose his rights to the property. Title insurance provides a financial backing to cover these types of scenarios and would not only defend the new owner, but would also provide financial compensation to the omitted heir and buy out his interest in the real property.

Another hidden defect is a deed or mortgage signed under duress or by a person without the capacity to execute the instrument. This scenario covers a minor executing a mortgage or deed in the chain of title or a person signing an instrument on behalf of a corporation or partnership who, it is subsequently discovered, did not have the authority to bind the entity. These types of fact-patterns are more common than most people think and they can create a complete failure of title. The new owner or lender would have little recourse after losing all of his interest in the property. Title insurance covers this "hidden" defect and overall, provides a degree of finality for each real estate transaction after closing.

Clearly, not all risks are shifted to the title insurance company, but these scenarios demonstrate that title insurance certainly provides the insured with a great benefit. It is important to read and understand the coverages afforded by a typical title policy to know what risks are shifted to the title insurance company. Owner's policies and lender's policies are similar in the type of coverage afforded. The standard policy jackets for each type of policy typically provide coverage against loss or damage sustained or incurred by the insured by reason of:

1. Title to the estate or interest being vested other than in the insured;
2. Any defect in or lien or encumbrance on the title;
3. Unmarketability of title; or
4. Lack of a right of access to and from the land.

Title to the estate being vested in other than the insured: This is perhaps the most easily understood coverage. It means that the insurer confirms that the insured is the lawful owner of the property above all other's claims. A title search will provide the most information regarding this coverage and it is the title agent's most important responsibility. A chain of title is compiled and a determination is made as to who must convey title to the property. It is also the title agent's responsibility to verify who would have the proper authority to sign on behalf of business entities that may have an interest in the subject property. In the event an error is made as to the proper party, the title insurance company will take the necessary steps to clear title and make any financial payouts to defend the insured's title.

Any defect in or lien or encumbrance on the title: This item protects against any lien or encumbrance affecting the title to a property. The most common of these is an outstanding mortgage. Surprisingly, this is typically the most common defect in title, based on the number of claims made in any given year. An insured, under a lender's policy, generally requires that their mortgage is a valid first mortgage superior to all other liens. When title to the property is examined, the title insurance company requires that all other liens or encumbrances be paid off prior to, or at closing. When they are not properly paid in full, the insured under either a lender or owner's policy may require that the lien be satisfied by the title insurance company. Prior to the advent of title insurance, the owner was required to bring a lawsuit against the seller and hope to collect the necessary sum to payoff the lien or encumbrance. Title insurance is an efficient remedy to handle this type of title defect.

Unmarketibility of title: Unmarketability of title is sometimes difficult to understand and define since it is typically left to the courts discretion to make such a decision. This language does not cover circumstances from the physical condition of the property, such as an undisclosed environmental contamination, but rather covers an apparent matter that would permit a reasonable person to have a certain amount of doubt as to the future marketability of the property to a subsequent person at the property's fair market value. A title defect can sometimes destroy the marketability of the property, but not all defects render title to the property as "unmarketable". For example, an easement running through the middle of the subject property may not be the most desirable location for the easement and the insured may file a claim that the title is "unmarketable". However, this fact alone does not make title unmarketable. Similarly, an encroachment from a neighbor's fence may become a title defect, but it may not rise to the level of making title to the property unmarketable. This coverage attempts to cover those items that do not clearly fall into the other specific categories of coverage, and this coverage allows the courts to have the ability to use this general provision of the title policy to make the insured whole by stating that the title to the property is "unmarketable" due to the specific defect raised by the insured. Again, without title insurance, the new owner's only recourse would be to file a lawsuit against the seller and attempt to collect sufficient funds from the seller to cover the expense of dealing with a particular title defect.

Lack of right of access to and from the land: This coverage provides the owner with an assurance that access exists to and from the property. This coverage is generally most useful for raw land, but it is obviously necessary for all types of property. Most subdivided neighborhoods will provide access for each property via public roads, however, this coverage does not require that all access to property be through a public road. For example, access may be derived from a permanent easement to another parcel of property and then to a public road. The right of access has also been interpreted to mean that access can be obtained from a yearly, renewable license to use another's property.

This coverage is also closely tied to the requirement that a proper survey be used in each transaction. Typically, the title agent does not visit the property prior to closing and therefore, relies on the survey to determine if the property has proper access, as well as determining

170

whether there are any other title defects raised by the condition and layout of the property. The surveyor enables the title agent to "see" the property and make these important determinations. While a survey is not required by every buyer, the title company will require a survey due to the coverage being afforded by the title policy.

By understanding the types of coverages afforded by a typical title policy, a buyer can make sure that the title is clear and satisfactory to the property being purchased. Moreover, by knowing the type of coverages available, a buyer or lender may determine that more assurances are needed, based on the type of property being purchased. Endorsements to the title policy are available for both owner's and lender's policies that provide the insured with an additional level of protection, depending on the type of property that is being insured.

Endorsements

The most common endorsement for lenders is the Form 9 Endorsement, also known as the Affirmative Coverage Endorsement. It provides the insured with additional assurances that the property is not in violation of any restrictions, easements or setback lines as established by the Plat of the property. This endorsement also provides coverage against encroachments onto the property or encroachments by any improvements of the property onto neighboring property, which may be forced to be removed at a later date. This endorsement is not automatically given and requires additional searches by the title agent to confirm that they may be given.

Another popular endorsement, the Environmental Protection Lien Endorsement, is required by lenders in almost all mortgage transactions. This endorsement provides coverage for the insured against loss or damage due to any environmental protection lien recorded prior to the insured mortgage. These liens are provided generally by state statute and may take priority over the insured mortgage even though they may be recorded apart from the public

171

property records. Generally, state statutes provide the parameters for these types of liens and only standard notices are recorded amongst the public records referencing a particular statute. Without further investigation, the lender's mortgage could be susceptible to a superior claim. Clearly, this is a coverage that lenders especially need to make certain that their mortgages are in first position.

The Condominium Endorsement, protects lenders against any violations of the condo rules or regulations that would result in forfeiture of title. The condominium association may file a lien against the property, which may be superior to the insured mortgage in the event the assessments have not been paid or if rules have been violated by the property owner. This coverage requires the title agent to do additional inquiry with the Condominium Association to determine if a lien may be filed pursuant to the condominium rules and regulation and what effect it may have on the insured mortgage. A similar endorsement exists for Homeowners' Associations, and is called the Planned Unit Development Endorsement. Both are valuable to the insured when the property is subject to the additional rules and regulations.

Another less common endorsement in residential transactions, but one that is commonly used in vacant land transactions is the Contiguity Endorsement. This endorsement provides affirmative coverage that two parcels of property are contiguous to one another without any gaps, gores, or hiatuses between them. This endorsement prevents a situation where a large tract of land made up of two parcels is purchased only to discover that a small strip of land in the middle of the two parcels is owned by another party. The Contiguity Endorsement is used in order to make certain that the two separate parcels are completely adjacent to one another from end to end without any gaps in the legal description.

Another common endorsement in residential developments is the Construction Loan Endorsement. This endorsement is used during a construction project and is sometimes referred to as a draw-down endorsement. It provides coverage throughout a construction project at different stages to provide protection against construction liens being filed during a project that can result in a forfeiture of title. By reviewing title at different points during a construction project, the lender can be assured that the project is being completed in a lien-free manner. In addition, the amount of coverage afforded by the title policy increases as the amount funded by the construction lender increases. This protects the construction lender's interest, dollar-for-dollar as additional funds are invested into the construction project.

Endorsements may also be used to provide additional coverage depending on the type of loan or property involved in the transaction.

The protection afforded by title insurance may be the least understood process in a real estate transaction for consumers. Buyers often do not realize what title insurance covers or how it provides protection. Lenders, however, realize the importance of title insurance in order to have a safety-net in the event a title claim arises. Clearly, title insurance has allowed the secondary market to grow and has provided additional loan funds to be available for home buyers. Buyers can obtain a sense of security knowing that in the event a problem arises in the chain of title, the title insurance company is available for protection. As with other types of insurance, the consumer should read and understand the coverages and exceptions provided in his title insurance policy in order to feel confident with his home purchase decision.

Homeowners Insurance
by
Maria Elena Cisneros

Fire policies, dwelling policies, personal multiple peril policies and homeowners policies are different ways of saying the same thing. They are all meant to cover private dwellings (designed for occupancy of 1 to 4 families) and their contents. This chapter will analyze the Homeowners Policy for owners of private residences and condominiums; that is, the insured must be the owner and occupant of the residence.

The Homeowner's Policy is structured to cover both tangible and the intangible. The policy is assembled as follows:

Homeowners-Section I
Coverage
> A - Dwelling or Building Property- Dwelling Extension
> B - Personal Property
> C - Loss of Use
> D - Loss Assessment
> L - Personal Liability - Damage to Property of Others
> M - Medical Payments to Others

These terms could leave a lot of questions for someone not versed in the specific language of the insurance world. Here is a simpler explanation.

Coverage A - Dwelling
The coverage afforded under "dwelling" is based on the residence structure and this should be insured at replacement cost value,

175

that is, the amount it would cost to replace the residence structure in today's market, not what it cost to build when it was originally built. This dwelling amount does not include the value of the land where the house is located. No matter what the damage to the structure is, even if it burns to the ground, the land will always have a value and will not disappear. Therefore, the price paid for a house is not necessarily the same amount the house is insured for. The insurance company will estimate the insurable value of the home based upon the square footage, building type (masonry, frame, etc.), year built, the type of roof, number of rooms and use of rooms (i.e. family room, formal dining room, library, bedrooms with adjoining bathrooms), type of floors (tile, marble, carpeting, wood) and overall finishes. Also, the location of the property is important since building costs differ in different areas of the country.

The replacement cost of the house can also be determined at the time the property appraisal is performed. The appraisal document has a section where the estimated value of the structure is indicated. The appraisal, as well as the value estimated by the insurance company, is not an exact science. It is an estimate of the value of the property.

Dwelling Extension

This section provides coverage of 10% of the dwelling amount to cover related structures on the premises when they are separated by a clear space. An example of a dwelling extension would be a separate garage or a separate structure not rented out to others. If it were rented to others a different kind of policy would apply.

Coverage B- Personal Property

All personal property usually found in the dwelling and belonging to the person named in the policy, and all residing members of the household is covered. The value assigned to the personal property is based on a percentage of the dwelling amount. This amount varies by policy type and ranges from 50% to 75% of the amount of the dwelling. In addition, there are specified limits of coverage on certain items, such as money, securities, passports, other documentation, firearms and jewelry. Under this section, there is also some coverage for Business Property located in the premises. There is usually a maximum limit of $2,500 for this coverage and certain restrictions apply. The limits of coverage for Personal Property can be found in the policy booklet.

Coverage C - Loss of Use

This is also referred to as Additional Living Expense which may be needed to maintain the normal standard of living if the property suffers damage by an insurable situation and the policyholder is unable to stay in the home. Coverage is limited to the shortest time needed to repair, replace or permanently relocate, but not to exceed a certain period of time established by the company (e.g. 12 months).

Coverage D - Loss Assessment

This pays for the insured's share of assessments charged by the association (if there is a homeowner's association) against all homeowners for a loss to property owned in common by all homeowners, such as common recreation areas, community walls, street lights, including personal property. Also, other situations may be covered such as damages the association may be obligated to pay. The scope of coverage varies among carriers.

Coverage L - Personal Liability- Damage to the property of others

Liability means legal responsibility. In a liability case, the other party, not the insured, would be the party receiving the benefit provided by this coverage. The basic coverage included in the policy is $100,000, but higher limits are available. Situations covered under this section would include an accident occurring in the insured's home where someone is injured due to some negligent act on the part of the homeowner, such as a dog biting incident, or similar mishap. Coverage is limited to $500 for any one occurrence for loss or damage to property of others when in the insured's custody. This is a common coverage found in Homeowner's Policies although not all companies offer it.

ADDITIONAL COVERAGE

Some policies offer the option to add or increase coverage in the policy. The most common options available are:

Jewelry and Furs
Silverware/Goldware Theft
Home Computers
Firearms
Business Property

ENDORSEMENTS - FLOATERS

Policies have limits for certain types of items insured under the policy, as explained previously. Within limits certain categories can be increased, and included in a Homeowner's Policy. The other option is to insure those items separately under a Personal Articles Floater. The most popular floater is for coverage of covers jewelry and furs.

The basic jewelry & fur coverage afforded under a Homeowner's Policy is $1,000. Some policies give the insured the option of increasing the jewelry and furs coverage up to $5,000 for an additional premium. If jewelry coverage in excess of the $5,000 maximum is needed, a Personal Article Floater or Jewelry Floater is the instrument by which this can be accomplished. Generally, the insurance company will request a recent appraisal or proof of purchase within the last two years showing the value of the items in order to insure the valuables. This is an inexpensive policy for those seeking additional coverage for jewelry and furs not provided under their Homeowner's Policy. Separate deductibles apply.

Personal Article Floaters

Floaters are also available for silverware/goldware, home computers, firearms, fine arts, musical instruments, cameras and collectible items. Consult with the insurance company to find out their requirements and conditions. Separate deductibles also apply to these policies.

ENDORSEMENTS

Endorsements are additional/optional coverages available under the policy for an additional premium. Some of these are as follows:

Replacement Cost on Contents

Usually, contents are covered in the policy at actual cash value. Replacement Cost coverage is an endorsement of great benefit to the insured in that it covers the contents without taking into account any depreciation of the item. For example, a television purchased ten years ago for $700 would be depreciated at the time of the claim and probably worth about $100 - that is the television's actual cash value. In order to replace the television, the insured would have to purchase a new television set. Replacement cost coverage would reimburse the insured the amount that it costs to buy a new television. The insurance company would reimburse the insured the difference between the actual cash value paid under the policy and the cost of the new television set (of like kind and quality) once the insured has replaced it.

Sewer Back-up

This endorsement will cover contents damaged due to back up of sewers and drains.

Building Ordinance

In many instances a building that has sustained substantial damage can only be repaired or replaced if the improvements are built to the building codes in effect at the time. Building codes are subject to periodic updating and structures built years ago may not be in compliance with the latest code changes. In areas where building codes are subject to changes, a policyholder may want to consider the benefits of this type of endorsement. This coverage is available at a 25% increase (50% available in some cases) of dwelling amount.

Earthquake and Wind Coverage Endorsements

Most homeowner policies do not cover damage caused by an earthquake, but coverage can be added to most policies as an endorsement for an additional premium. The cost varies depending on the insurance company and on several factors such as age of structure, risk of likelihood of an earthquake, amount of coverage and deductible. Areas such as California, Washington and Alaska are places where earthquake insurance is particularly applicable, but there are other areas of the country where earthquake insurance is recommended.

Windstorm coverage, which is a strong concern in coastal areas such as Florida, Louisiana, Texas and the Carolinas, is provided as an endorsement to the Homeowner's Policy at an additional cost. The dwelling location is key since properties located close to the coast may require a completely separate policy to provide wind protection instead of having an endorsement added to the regular Homeowner's Policy.

DEDUCTIBLES

An integral part of every policy is the amount of the deductible. The deductible is that portion of the loss that the insured retains and it is always applied to the loss first. Deductibles come in all sizes, from $100 to $10,000 or more. The tendency in recent years has been to have higher deductibles, but it really depends on the insured's desire and financial circumstances. The lower the deductible, the higher the premium. In certain high-risk areas of the country, insurance companies have separated deductibles in two sections: Hurricane Deductible and Other Perils.

Hurricane Deductible

Hurricane Deductibles are usually expressed as a percentage of the dwelling amount although a $500 deductible is available for homes insured under $99,999. The most common hurricane deductibles available are 2% and 5%, and for higher valued homes up to 10% is available. The key word here is "as a percentage of the dwelling amount." If a home is insured for $200,000 with a 5% hurricane deductible, that means the policyholder will be responsible for the first $10,000 of the claim. The different options should be examined carefully before deciding upon which to select. As was mentioned earlier, the higher the deductible the lower the premium, and in the case of the hurricane deductible as in other Homeowner's Policies, a higher deductible means more out of pocket expense to the policyholder.

Other Peril Deductible

Other Peril means the deductible applicable for losses due to occurrences other than by wind or earthquake such as fire, theft or lightning. The most common deductibles are usually $500, $1,000 and $2,000, but deductibles up to $5,000 and higher are available.

DISCOUNTS

The types of discounts and the credits given vary depending on the insurance company. Not all companies offer the same discounts. Below are some of the most commonly offered discounts.

Home Alert Discount

This discount varies depending on the degree of protection,

from simple smoke detectors to sophisticated burglar alarm systems connected to a central reporting station.

Windstorm Loss Reduction

Hurricane Shutters that conform to the Building Code and are inspected by the county where property is located will help qualify a homeowner for the Windstorm Loss Reduction discount. This discount also varies depending on whether all openings, including the garage, are protected or if only the windows have the protection. Impact resistant windows within code specifications also qualify for this discount.

ADDITIONAL CHARGES

Just as discounts are given based on certain situations, so are charges imposed. Each company has different rules, but there are certain charges that are found regardless of the company insuring the property.

Utility Rating

Dwellings over 30 years old whose electrical, heating and plumbing has not been updated are surcharged. As a general rule, insurance companies refuse to insure homes over 50 years old that have not had their electrical, heating and plumbing updated. Certificates of Compliance from licensed companies must be presented to the insurance company in order to obtain insurance coverage in such instances.

Loss History

Claims history is a very important part of the underwriting process. Prior loss history is taken into account and a surcharge may be applied if there is a high claim frequency. Hurricane losses are usually not considered part of the claim frequency since it is an unavoidable situation.

FLOOD INSURANCE

National Flood Insurance Program (NFIP) coverage is available to all owners of insurable property in a community participating in the program. Almost all of the nation's communities with serious threat of flooding participate in the NFIP. The Federal Emergency Management Association (FEMA) publishes maps indicating a community's flood hazard areas and the degree of risk in those areas. Insurance agencies offering flood policies have access to these maps and can advise property owners if their property is in a Special Flood Hazard Area. For properties in Special Flood Hazard Areas, the mortgage company will require a flood policy to be in effect at the time of closing. The policy provides protection for both dwelling and contents.

CONDOMINIUM UNIT OWNER'S POLICY

This policy is for the individual condominium unit owner who owns and occupies, at least for a portion of the year, a unit located in the building owned and insured by a condominium association, a townhome association, a cooperative, a homeowner association or any other similar association. The above listed associations carry insurance on the structure and the property in the building owned by the unit owners in common. Each individual owner is free to insure his own unit as he sees fit. If the condominium unit is rented to others for longer than six months, this policy would be inappropriate. It would not qualify for the Personal Lines of Insurance.

The unit owner shares with all other unit owners the land where the building is located and the common areas such as entrances, exits, elevators, hallways, recreation areas and roof. Each unit, together with its common interest, is described as real property.

Section I

Coverage:

A- Building Property

B- Personal Property

C- Loss of Use

D- Loss Assessment

Section II

Coverage

L- Personal Liability- Damage to Property of Others

M- Medical Payments to Others

Coverage A- Building Prpoerty

The coverage provided under Building Property pertains to items such as building additions and alterations, installations and improvements comprising a part of the unit. This section covers interior walls, bathroom fixtures, bathroom and kitchen cabinets, carpeting or any other improvements made to the unit.

Coverage B- Personal Property

All personal property usually found in the unit and belonging to the person named in the policy and all residing members of the household is covered. The amount of coverage provided is based on the estimated replacement cost of the contents. Insurance companies have calculators where they can help the insured estimate the amount of insurance they should carry based on the square footage of the unit and the quality of the contents (economy, standard, luxury).

Coverage C- Loss of Use

This is also referred to as Additional Living Expense. If a loss causes the residence premises to become uninhabitable, this coverage will provide the necessary increase in cost to maintain the insured's standard of living. Coverage in limited to the shortest time needed to repair, replace or permanently relocate, but not to exceed a certain period of time established in the policy (e.g. 12 months).

Coverage D- Loss Assessment

This pays for the insured's share of assessments charged by the association against all unit owners for a loss to property owned in common, such as common recreation areas, community walls, street lights, including personal property. Also other situations may be covered such as damages the association is obligated to pay.

Coverage L- Personal Liability

Personal liability coverage protects the insured if a claim is made or a suit is brought against an insured for damages because of bodily injury or property damage caused by a negligent act of the insured. The basic coverage included is $100,000, but higher limits are available.

Coverage M- Medical Payments to Others

This provides coverage for necessary medical expenses incurred because of accidental bodily injury to a person on the resident premises of the insured. In addition, coverage may apply in certain circumstances even if a person is off the resident premises. Not all companies offer the same protection, therefore a person seeking Coverage M should inquire about it when purchasing a policy.

ENDORSEMENTS

The endorsements offered under the condominium Unit Owner's Policy are basically the same as those listed under the Homeowner's Policy. Some insurance companies offer certain uncommon endorsements such as Vacancy Coverage, Rented Personal Property and Waterbed Liability.

ADDITIONAL COVERAGE

The same basic coverage is offered as in the Homeowner's Program, as follows:

Silverware/Goldware Theft
Home Computers
Firearms
Business Property

Private Mortgage Insurance
by
Don Rosenthal

What Is Private MI?

Traditionally, lenders have required a down payment of at least 20 percent of a home's value. For most first-time home buyers, saving money for such a sizeable down payment is the greatest barrier to home ownership. Lenders will approve a mortgage with a smaller down payment, however, if the mortgage is covered by Private MI.

Private MI, also known as mortgage guaranty insurance, protects a lender if a homeowner defaults on a loan. Lenders generally require mortgage insurance on low down payment loans because studies show that a borrower with less than 20 percent invested in a house is more likely to default on a mortgage. In effect, the mortgage insurance company shares the risk of foreclosure with the lender. Low down payment loans are also referred to as high-ratio loans (loan-to-value ratio), indicating the relationship between the amount of the mortgage loan and the value of the property. The home buyer and the mortgage insurer share a common interest in the mortgage financing transaction because they each stand to lose in the event of default. The borrower will lose the home and the equity invested in it, and the mortgage insurer will have to pay the lender's claim on the defaulted loan. Thus, both the insurer and the borrower are concerned that the home is affordable not only at the time of purchase, but throughout the years of home ownership.

Private MI is the private-sector alternative to non-conventional, government-insured home loans. Mortgages backed by the government are insured by the Federal Housing Administration or guaranteed by the Department of Veterans Affairs. Generally, home buyers must make a down payment of at least 3 to 5 percent of a home's value to be considered for Private MI. However, qualified borrowers with excellent credit standing can be approved for a mortgage loan with less than 3 percent down. Private MI is available on a wide variety of conventional mortgages, including most fixed and adjustable rate home loans, giving borrowers the freedom to choose the type of loan that best suits their needs.

Private MI should not be confused with mortgage life insurance, which pays an outstanding mortgage debt if the borrower holding the insurance policy dies.

Meeting the Affordability Challenge

Affordability continues to be the nation's most pressing housing problem, and the mortgage insurance industry plays a vital role in helping low and moderate income families become homeowners. Mortgage insurance aids affordability because it allows families to buy homes with less cash. A home purchase can be made years sooner with Private MI.

Over two-thirds of the families in the United States own their own homes, but a look at the rate of home ownership broken down by income levels reveals an interesting picture. Home ownership in America is skewed toward those with household incomes of more than $50,000.

Statistics show that high-income households constitute a clear minority of U.S. households and that most people in these categories already own homes. In 1999, only 11 percent of U.S. households had incomes over $100,000, and 91 percent of them owned homes. Six percent of households earned $80,000 to $100,000, and 88 percent owned homes. Twenty percent had incomes between $50,000 and $80,000, and 80 percent owned homes. In contrast, 63 percent of households had incomes below $50,000, but only 57 percent owned homes.

Private Insurers Step in to Help

For years, members of the Mortgage Insurance Companies of America (MICA) have worked with the secondary market agencies, mortgage lenders, and local consumer groups across the country to identify ways to better serve low and moderate income home buyers. These partnerships have increased the mortgage insurance industry's awareness of the unique needs of borrowers at the local level. They also have helped motivate individual insurers to develop special programs with flexible underwriting guidelines to help low and moderate income families qualify for financing. These programs demonstrate that by working together, communities, lenders, insurers, and investors can expand home ownership opportunities for low and moderate income families.

Many of the new programs' features have been so successful that they now are used in all types of mortgage transactions, not just those targeted for low and moderate income families. One of the most popular features is the use of alternative credit verification methods. For instance, a record of prompt utility bill and rent payments can be substituted for the traditional credit report to establish a potential borrower's credit.

A Financial Industry Success Story

The modern Private MI industry was born in the 1950's, but the industry's roots go back to the late 1800's and the founding of title insurance companies in New York. The state passed the first legislation authorizing the insuring of mortgages in 1904. In 1911, the law was expanded to allow title insurance companies to buy and resell mortgages, comparable to today's secondary mortgage market. To make loans more marketable, companies offered guarantees of payment as well as title, thus establishing the business of mortgage insurance. In addition to insuring mortgages, companies began offering participations, or mortgage bonds. These bonds allowed multiple investors to hold a mortgage or group of mortgages.

During the 1920's, rising real estate prices allowed most foreclosed properties to be sold at a profit, and more than 50 mortgage insurance companies flourished in New York. Since mortgage insurance was considered a low-risk business, the firms were virtually unregulated and thinly capitalized. Most had little experience with sound credit underwriting. This situation went relatively unnoticed until the Great Depression. With the catastrophic collapse of real estate values in the 1930's, New York's entire mortgage insurance industry folded. As a result, the governor commissioned a study to examine the problems that had developed in mortgage lending and insurance. The study, known as the Alger Report, recommended prohibiting conflicts of interest, setting stringent capital and reserve requirements, and adopting sound appraisal, investment, and accounting procedures. The report became a blueprint for a strong post-World War II mortgage insurance industry built on new regulations and financial structures. The industry's sound regulatory and financial foundation has ensured that even during difficult economic times, lenders are able to continue making low down payment loans backed by mortgage insurance.

FHA Lends a Hand

During the Depression, the need to stimulate housing construction by encouraging mortgage investment became evident. The federal government entered the mortgage insurance business in 1934 with the creation of the Federal Housing Administration. With its promise of full repayment to lenders if borrowers defaulted on their home loans, the FHA home loan insurance program created new confidence in mortgage instruments and stimulated investment in housing.

To direct government assistance to those most in need, the FHA imposed ceilings on the insurable loan amount for single-family homes.

After World War II, the government's mortgage insurance role expanded with a Veterans Affairs mortgage guarantee program to help veterans in their transition to civilian life. The FHA and VA insurance programs have helped stimulate the housing market for several decades.

The Private Sector Emerges

In 1957, a Milwaukee lawyer named Max Karl founded the first modern Private MI company, Mortgage Guaranty Insurance Corp., making the conventional low down payment mortgage a viable product for mortgage lenders. A regulatory structure for Private MI was established that included strong conflict of interest provisions and a one line-of-business structure to ensure that mortgage insurers' reserves would not be mixed with reserves for other lines of insurance. In addition, a unique contingency reserve structure and capital requirements were established to recognize the catastrophic nature of mortgage default risk and prevent companies from entering the mortgage insurance business without long-term commitments. This regulatory framework provided a foundation for establishing additional Private MI companies.

Housing's Heyday

The 1960's saw expansion of the modern Private MI industry, followed by dramatic growth in the early 1970's in conjunction with the emerging dominance of the secondary mortgage market. All mortgages originate in the primary mortgage market. In the secondary mortgage market, existing mortgages are bought, sold, and traded to other lenders, government agencies, or investors.

The federal government chartered two special-purpose organizations to enhance the availability and uniformity of mortgage credit across the nation. Those organizations, the Federal National Mortgage Association (Fannie Mae) and the Federal Home Loan

Mortgage Corp. (Freddie Mac), provide direct links between the primary mortgage markets and the nation's capital markets. Fannie Mae, a government-sponsored but privately owned corporation established in 1938, creates mortgage-backed securities backed by FHA, VA and conventional loans. Freddie Mac, created in 1970, is structured and operates in a manner similar to Fannie Mae.

The demand by mortgage investors for investment-quality mortgage loans expanded the need for mortgage credit enhancement. Indeed, the Fannie Mae and Freddie Mac charters require that they carry one of three forms of credit enhancement on low down payment loans they purchase, one of which is Private MI. The Private MI industry has helped fill this credit enhancement role, enabling Fannie Mae and Freddie Mac to buy and securitize low down payment conventional loans. As a result, loans secured with minimal down payments steadily increased as a percentage of total mortgage originations.

Secondary market purchases of low down payment loans helped fuel the tremendous expansion in home construction and sales during the 1970's and '80's, aiding many first-time and other home buyers. Privately insured mortgage loans became an increasingly important part of the mortgage finance system.

Put to the Test

The 1980's wrote a new chapter in the history of mortgage insurance. The challenge of the early '80's was helping homeowners, lenders, real estate agents, and builders cope with double-digit interest rates and inflation in a period of severe recession. To help qualify more borrowers, conventional low down payment loans were paired with experimental adjustable-rate mortgages and features such as initially discounted "teaser rates," negative amortization, and graduated payment increases. By 1984, more than half of all insured mortgage loans had down payments of less than 10 percent, and many of these were adjustable-rate mortgages.

As economic conditions deteriorated, particularly in energy oriented regions of the country, defaults began to rise, resulting in numerous foreclosures. The mortgage insurance industry paid more than $6 billion in claims to its policyholders during the 1980's.

Policyholders included commercial banks, savings institutions, institutional mortgage investors, mortgage bankers, Federal Deposit Insurance Corp., Federal Savings and Loan Insurance Corp., Fannie Mae, and Freddie Mac. Mortgage insurance protected all these mortgage and capital providers from extensive losses on high-ratio loans. Even in the prosperous economic times of the 1990's, the mortgage insurance industry paid more than $8 billion in claims, once again demonstrating its ability to function as designed in both good and bad economic climates.

Looking Ahead

Only third-party insurers can effectively disperse risk nationally, collecting premiums in strong markets while supporting policyholders in weaker markets. The unique and stringent capital and catastrophic loss reserve requirements that mortgage insurers must maintain passed the test of severe economic stress during the 1980's. The high level of claim payments made by the Private MI industry during that period, coupled with its continued financial health, proved that lenders and investors can rely on mortgage insurance for credit enhancement and default protection.

The Private MI industry emerged from the 1980's financially strong and well positioned to meet the needs of the nation's home buyers, mortgage lenders, and mortgage investors through the 1990's and on into the new century.

How Mortgage Insurance Works

The purpose of mortgage insurance is to protect lenders from default-related losses on conventional first mortgages made to home buyers who make down payments of less than 20 percent of the purchase price. Without mortgage insurance, lenders would suffer significant losses on defaulting loans with high loan-to-value ratios. Many expenses accompany a default. Interest charges accumulate during the delinquent period, as well as during foreclosure, a period that can total a year or more. Other costs include legal fees, home maintenance and repair expenses, real estate brokers' fees and other closing costs. These costs generally total 15 percent or more of the loan amount. Another frequent loss occurs when the foreclosed property is resold for less than its original sales price.

Private MI companies insure against the losses associated with defaulted loans by guaranteeing payment to the lender of the top 20 to 30 or more percent of the claim amount. One of the mortgage insurer's key roles is to act as a review underwriter for credit and collateral risks related to individual loans, as well as for local, regional, and national economic risks that could increase the loss from mortgage defaults.

Recognizing the near certainty of losses on most foreclosures, the major investors who supply liquidity to the mortgage market, such as Fannie Mae and Freddie Mac, require credit enhancements such as mortgage insurance on all low down payment loans. The two agencies generally require that mortgages with loan-to-value ratios higher than 80 percent have insurance coverage on the amount of the loan greater than 70 percent of value.

The Claims Process

The type and amount of coverage selected by the lender determine how much the private mortgage insurer will pay if the borrower defaults and the lender must foreclose. The claim amount filed with the mortgage insurer generally includes principal and delinquent interest due on the loan, legal expenses incurred during foreclosure, the expense of maintaining the home, and any advances the lender made to pay taxes or insurance. Private mortgage insurers have increasingly sought to intervene and help counsel borrowers if they happen to hit a rough patch in their financial life and are seeking solutions to avoid foreclosure. Over the years, thousands of homeowners have benefitted from this kind of assistance and have protected their credit rating.

Generally, after a lender has instituted foreclosure and has acquired title to the property, it can submit a claim to the insurance company. The insurer has two options to satisfy the claim:

1. Pay the lender the entire claim amount and take title to the property.
2. Pay the percentage of coverage of the total claim amount stated in the policy (generally 20 to 30 percent) and let the lender retain title to the property.

Before making a decision, an insurer generally will try to determine the potential resale price of the property and the expenses resulting from the resale, including the real estate agent's commission and other settlement costs. A more detailed description of how mortgage insurance operates is contained in the master policies of individual companies. Master policies, which differ from company to company, are contracts issued to lenders that formally set out the conditions of the insurance. They define the procedures lenders must follow to insure a loan, what to do if borrowers become delinquent on their payments, and how to make a claim. They also define how the lender and the insurer must manage mortgage default risk. Master policies are tailored to individual state regulations and incorporate the rights and responsibilities of the policyholder and the insurer.

Managing Risk in a Volatile Environment

The business environment changes constantly, and mortgage insurance is no exception. Deregulation of financial services, globalization of the economy, increased securitization of mortgage products, and various legislative initiatives have increased the risk of mortgage lending for lenders, insurers, and investors.

The major factors on which mortgage default risk is based include:
1. Size of the down payment.
2. Potential for property appreciation or depreciation.
3. Borrower's credit history.

Other risk factors include:
1. Purpose of the loan.
2. Type of mortgage instrument.
3. Whether the borrower will occupy the home.
4. Interest rate.

The most unpredictable risk factor, by far, is the stability of the property's value. Mortgage insurers constantly monitor local, regional, and national economic conditions. By studying population and employment growth, the supply of existing housing, housing starts, and other economic factors, insurers can better evaluate the sensitivity of local economies to downturns as well as upturns.

Long-Term Protection

Risk management is vital to the long-term protection of policy holders' reserves because of the unique nature of mortgage default risk. The risk cycle for mortgage insurance is significantly longer than for other property-casualty insurance products. Although lenders may decide to cancel insurance when the default risk has been sufficiently reduced, coverage and risk can run for many years.

Mortgage insurance remains renewable at the option of the insured lender or investor and at the renewal rate quoted when the policy commitment was issued. Mortgage insurers cannot raise premiums or cancel policies if risk increases over time. Because mortgage insurers make a long-term commitment on each loan they insure, a long-term risk management perspective is essential to protect policyholders' interests.

Risk Dispersion

Mortgage insurance helps lenders and investors balance the short-term need for increased mortgage originations with the long-term need for investment-quality business. Mortgage insurers offer the risk dispersion and pooling of risk that few individual mortgage lenders or investors could accomplish on their own.

Geographic Distribution.

Mortgage insurers operate on a national basis, which provides the geographic dispersion necessary to protect policyholders during regional economic cycles.

Temporal Distribution.

Mortgage insurance also provides a reserve system that accumulates policyholders' reserves over time. Under today's business conditions, it is not possible for individual lenders and investors to accumulate similar reserves.

Loan-to-Value Distribution.

Because risk increases as the loan-to-value ratio increases, mortgage insurers seek to balance their mix of 95 percent, 90 percent, and lower loan-to-value ratio loans. The mortgage insurance industry's sound underwriting and risk-dispersion practices serve to produce higher-quality originations for mortgage lenders and higher-quality investments for investors.

The Expanding Market for Mortgage Insurance

The market for mortgage insurance changed dramatically during the 1980's, resulting in a much stronger, healthier mortgage insurance industry in the 1990's. The industry overcame many problems that hampered it in the '80's, including increased self-insurance, restructuring within the industry, and uncertain economic conditions.

The industry's volume of business continued to grow through the 1990's. A number of factors contributed to the industry's success, including:

1. Increased industry presence in the low and moderate income market.
2. Increased lending in inner cities.
3. Enhanced marketing efforts by individual companies and the industry as a whole.
4. Single-digit interest rates drawing first-time home buyers into the market.
5. Greater public awareness of the availability of Private MI.
6. Greater emphasis on the use of mortgage insurance as a credit enhancement to meet risk-based capital requirements for banks and savings institutions.
7. Increased use of mortgage insurance by trade-up buyers for tax benefits, since mortgage interest remains deductible.

FHA's Role

FHA, VA, and private mortgage insurers play similar roles in making housing more affordable. Private MI is basically the private-sector alternative to FHA insurance, but there are several differences between the two.

Under federal law, Private MI on most loans originated on or after July 29, 1999, will terminate automatically once the mortgage is paid down to 78 percent of the original purchase price of the house. Unlike FHA, Private MI companies do not insure the total loan balance. The mortgage insurance industry shares the risk of default with the financial institution, the secondary market investor, and the homeowner. Sharing the risk provides incentive for all parties to keep the loan payments current. In addition, Private MI generally costs less than FHA insurance and is available on a wider variety of mortgage loan products; and, it is not subject to maximum loan amounts.

Cancellation and the Law:
The Homeowners Protection Act

Private MI makes it possible for potential home buyers to become homeowners sooner, for less money down. Federal law assures consumers that they can enjoy the benefits of Private MI, knowing that lenders will cancel it when it is no longer needed. The law includes two basic consumer protections:

1. It requires lenders to inform home buyers-both at closing and annually-about their right to request cancellation.
2. It requires lenders to automatically cancel insurance for those who do not request cancellation.

Even without the law, Private MI generally is cancelable once the homeowner builds up enough equity in the home. Investors set their own cancellation requirements. The mortgage insurance company does not make the decision to cancel insurance.

How the Law Works

The law is designed to demystify the Private MI cancellation process in the following ways:

1. Initial Disclosure. For loans originated on or after July 29, 1999, lenders must give borrowers a written notice at closing that explains they have Private MI on their mortgage and that they have the right to have it canceled at a certain point.

2. Annual Disclosure. Lenders must send borrowers an annual reminder that they have Private MI and have the right to request cancellation once they've met cancellation requirements. This requirement applies to all loans with cancelable Private MI, not just those obtained after July 29, 1999.

3. Borrower-Initiated Cancellation. For most loans originated on or after July 29, 1999, a lender must cancel Private MI at the request of a borrower whose mortgage balance is 80 percent of the original value of the house. The borrower must be up to date on mortgage payments and have no other loans on the house. The lender must be satisfied that the property value has not declined.

4. Automatic termination. For most insured loans originated on or after July 29,1999, Private MI will be canceled automatically when the mortgage balance is at 78 percent of the original value of the house. The borrower must be up to date on mortgage payments. Otherwise, insurance will be canceled automatically once the borrower becomes current. Exception: For mortgages defined as high risk, the lender will automatically cancel the Private MI at the mid-point of the loan. On a 30-year mortgage, for example, insurance will be canceled after 15 years.

Mortgage Pool Insurance Explained

In addition to insuring individual mortgage loans, mortgage insurers insure pools of mortgages. Mortgages are pooled so they can be sold in the secondary market and can receive an investment grade rating. Securities backed by mortgages are a significant tool for attracting capital to home financing, especially for the riskier loans. Pools can be formed with loans that may or may not have primary insurance. In most cases, pool insurance includes a liability limit for the mortgage insurer of 5 to 25 percent of the original principal balance of the mortgage pool. For example, a $10 million pool could incur default losses of $500,000 to $2.5 million without loss to the investor.

A Financially Healthy Industry

A strong indicator of the mortgage insurance industry's financial health is the combined ratio, which is the percentage of a company's premium income that it pays out in claims and expenses. The lower the ratio, the better the industry's underwriting performance and profitability. This is a result of sound underwriting and risk dispersion, as well as advanced market analysis, risk-monitoring programs, and management reports. In addition, the industry's expense ratio has remained nearly steady for two decades, reflecting the industry's ability to limit expenses.

For the past dozen years, the combined ratio has remained consistently profitable, and the industry has recorded a positive income from underwriting. Key measures of the industry's financial health all point toward the same conclusion: The mortgage insurance industry has been consistently profitable in the 1990's and is successfully building its reserves to pay future claims. The industry's profitability as a result of strong risk management. It is important to note that industry trends are aggregate numbers and that individual companies' results will vary. The claims-paying ability ratings of individual mortgage insurance companies are available from bond rating agencies.

Financial Strength of the System

Recent trends in industry profitability provide a graphic picture of the cyclical risks of mortgage lending. It is against this pattern of peaks and valleys that mortgage insurance was designed to protect lenders. The backbone of the industry's financial strength is its unique reserve system. This system is designed to enable the industry to withstand a sustained period of heavy defaults arising from serious regional or national economic downturns, as well as routine defaults and claims that occur normally throughout the cycle. Under the system, mortgage insurers are required to maintain three separate reserves to ensure adequate resources to pay claims:

Contingency reserves, required by law, protect policyholders against the type of catastrophic loss that can occur during a depressed economic period. Half of each premium dollar earned goes into the contingency reserve and cannot be touched by the mortgage insurance company for a 10-year period unless losses in a calendar year exceed 35 percent of earned premiums, depending on the state. Contingency reserves allow insurers to build reserves during the valley of the risk cycle to cover claims during peak years.

Case-basis loss reserves are established for losses on individual policies when the insurer is notified of defaults and foreclosures. This reserve account also includes a reserve for losses incurred but not reported.

Premiums received for the term of a policy are placed in unearned premium reserves. Each state establishes the method by which premiums are earned to match premiums with loss and exposure.

Fannie Mae, Freddie Mac, and Wall Street analysts closely monitor the industry's financial strength and have a keen financial interest in the industry's long-term health. Assets and reserves are important elements in measuring the industry's claims-paying ability.

A Growing Capital Base

Mortgage insurers operate within a conservative risk-to-capital ratio, with capital guidelines established by state insurance departments. Mortgage insurers must operate within a 25-to-1 ratio of risk to capital, which means they set aside $1 of capital for every $25 of risk they insure. Insured risk is defined as the percentage of each loan covered by an insurance policy. By adhering to such strict criteria, mortgage insurers have been able to guarantee a continued source of capital for home buying, even in difficult times.

Reinsurance-insuring the risk of one insurance company (the reinsured) by another company (the reinsurer)-helps a company reduce its loss exposure. Under a reinsurance agreement, the reinsurer participates proportionally in the reinsured's premium and potential losses. State regulations normally do not allow mortgage insurers to write insurance coverage of more than 25 percent on any individual loan amount. If an insurer wishes to offer coverage above 25 percent, it must reinsure the additional portion so another company holds the risk.

Rating agencies use financial models that specify a level of loss tolerance for a mortgage insurance company to ensure that adequate funds will be available over time to cover claims. The evaluation of capital adequacy for individual mortgage insurers is typically conducted on the basis of depression-level projected losses.

Industry Outlook: Enhancing Home ownership Opportunities

The United States continues to enjoy a robust and vibrant housing market. Interest rates remain in the single digits, many properties are available, and a wide range of financing options exists. Combined, these factors make it an opportune time for first time home buyers to enter the market and for trade-up buyers to make their move. As more people become homeowners, many will take advantage of Private MI to buy a home with a low down payment. Since 1992, about a million families a year have used mortgage insurance to become homeowners. Mortgage insurers are continually creating new ways to reach out to low-income borrowers, helping more families access the mortgage market and providing more opportunities for expanding home ownership. The Mortgage Insurance Companies of America (MICA) will continue its role of helping the industry anticipate opportunities to enhance home ownership and explain the benefits of low down payment financing to the public.

Part VI

Indispensable Tools for the Mortgage Banker

Quality Control in Mortgage Originations
by
James C. Hagan

The impact that fraud has on the mortgage industry has continued to grow significantly in the past five years. Today, fraud is not just the father falsifying a salary to help his son obtain a house he plans to live in. Schemes and major fraud are on the rise and can cost a lender or purchaser of the loan serious money. Failure of a lender to recognize and deal with fraud, improper disclosures, and other serious issues can be very costly. Take a loan where a property has been flipped until its collateral value is only 65% of the actual loan balance. Now a lender is faced with a possible buy-back of that loan from an upstream purchaser and a further loss from foreclosure and the resulting REO. If a lender is caught up in a scheme involving several loans, the loss can become devastating.

Compliance with lending regulations is imperative. Improper disclosures or failure to properly give a Right of Rescission may lead to significant refunds or extension of time for the borrower to opt out of the transaction. If a lender is audited by a regulatory agency such as the Office of the Comptroller of the Currency, or some state regulatory agency, and there are improper disclosures, fees, or disclosure calculations, these can result in the lender being required to do a complete audit of all loans to discover similar errors, and then to write checks to the borrowers to reimburse for the errors. Although many times the amount of a single check is not significant, the number of events and the cost to audit all loans made during a prescribed period of time causes the event to be a significant expense.

Automated Underwriting Systems ("AUS") do not do away with the need for quality control as some lenders believe. The automated process is only as good as the integrity of the data provided to the program. The data must be valid and the AUS requirements or findings followed to provide a loan that satisfies the ultimate purchaser of that loan. In selling an AUS loan to one of the GSEs ("Government Sponsored Entities" - Fannie Mae or Freddie Mac), a loan that receives less than an "Accept" or "Approved Eligible" status should be scrutinized very closely. Loans that do not fit these parameters may be considered less than "A" paper and be subject to risk based pricing.

Verification and investigation, either prior to or closely after the loan closing, can often identify issues before they reach a devastating outcome. The quality control department can make a big difference in the bottom line and in a company's future. But doing quality control has its cost along with its benefits.

While some lenders look at quality control as only a cost, others look at it as a cost savings center. It takes experienced personnel with the right tools to do the job, neither of which is inexpensive. On the other hand, a bad loan can mean a lender has to suffer a costly foreclosure, a possible buy-back, or an REO. There are lenders who track and reward their personnel based on the quality of the product produced.

Businesses must look at the manufacturing process to determine the number and severity of the defects, and how those defects can be addressed to make the process better. Mortgage lending is no different.

Mortgage loan quality control is often seen only as a paper work review. The process determines issues without the analysis of the frequency and severity of the issues discovered during the process. The person doing the audit often does not have use of the right tools to discover problems. In dealing with quality issues the lender must take time to investigate, analyze, and classify the findings based on the severity of the findings. A good QC program will allow the QC manager to slice and dice the findings, drill down to the heart of issues found and determine their origin.

Some areas of concentration in dealing with the findings are:

- The point in the process where issues arise.
- The severity of problem issues defined.
- Risk Analysis -- Are the issues found of a severity to cause a repurchase of the loan or a loss on an REO?
- Can the issues found be corrected?
- Has the company developed and implemented a sound quality control plan with a review of its effectiveness and the backing of management?
- Attention to the issues found at a management level high enough to be effective in dealing with the issues.
- Review of the quality control audit findings to look for trends.

Quality Control is often viewed as insignificant to the lenders production process. The results of the QC process, although reported to management, get lost or pushed back in the day-to-day effort to move forward to produce and/or to purchase more loans. The end result for the company can be costly when quality is sacrificed for volume or any other reason. A great side benefit to quality control is it allows a review of the company's file control system to see if notes and documents are being handled expeditiously. Failures in document control can lead to lost documents or lost files and may disrupt shipping of those loans to meet commitment deadlines.

Areas of production abuse seem to remain constant, so verifying some facts up front can save a lot of money later. The common areas of abuse or fraud are:

- Fraudulent gift letters
- Income verifications falsified or distorted
- Verifications of Deposit falsified

- Fraudulent bank statements
- Appraisals with false comparables or improper adjustments made to justify a highly inflated value.
- Flips - property is acquired and re-sold in a very short time frame, often to a related party.
- Sending verifications to P.O. Boxes or unsubstantiated addresses.
- Use of residential addresses for certain verifications.
- "Straw buyers" - Using someone as a buyer to obtain a loan only to facilitate a transfer of the property either away from a builder or to someone who otherwise would not qualify for the loan.
- Improper use of social security numbers.
- Improper data input to automated underwriting systems.
- High-tech also benefits those with criminal intent who can scan and produce near perfect documents.

Today's high-tech tools allow a better opportunity to catch fraud and misrepresentation. Some of these tools are expensive and complex databases accessed through the internet and only through a password protected subscription account. These types of tools are generally employed by very large lenders or outsource QC vendors who can justify the cost of the subscription by spreading that cost across a large number of loans or client lenders. Other tools are free Internet databases and CD phone disks that are available at many computer outlets. As the Internet continues to evolve more and more database tools are also evolving, so it pays to be vigilant in staying abreast of technology.

- Prior to funding, designate someone to make the calls that may save a company tens of thousands of dollars by simply re-verifying pieces of information. Research and re-verification done during the application process, or just before closing, can result in finding a problem before the loan is funded. Once the money is gone, so is much of the leverage to correct the problem.

- Prior to drafting a quality control plan, a lender should assess if it is best to use in-house personnel, or an outsource provider of QC services. Each of these solutions has different implications. The in-house department would be more of a fixed expense with the outsource provider being a variable expense with fees based on the number of files audited each month.

Suggestions for building a good QC plan include the following:

- Make a phone call regarding any suspect documents.
- Check the disbursements on the HUD-1 (check fees collected against disclosures, payoff of prior liens, and to see that the balance of proceeds went to the party shown as owner on the lender's title commitment.)
- A compliance check to see that RESPA and Truth-in-Lending disclosures are made properly and timely.
- Check to see that any state required disclosures are made.
- Use of the phone book, directory assistance, internet databases, or CD phone disk to check addresses or phone numbers.
- Check the documents for authenticity and check signatures against other signatures in the file from the same person.
- Checking for round numbers on employment or bank data.
- Do a data integrity check on automated underwriting submissions.
- Check the FICA tax calculations on payroll information.
- Check the social security numbers being used to determine who may be using them and when the number was issued. (The book

Profit Protection, Inc., explains the numbering system used and when numbers were issued, or not. Also check the website at: www.ssa.gov for further information from the Social Security Administration)

- IRS forms 4506 and 8821 allow verification of income reported to IRS.
- Good common sense -- The lender should ask: "Is the document being viewed logical based on the other loan facts before the lender?"
- If available, certain database checks could also be run to look at property values, location, existence and ownership of employers.
- Require written responses from parties responsible for serious defects or issues found.
- Trend minor issues to determine if a response or training is needed to address the issues.
- Have someone with authority to do follow-up on issues identified as possibly fraudulent.

QC issues that are minor often come from lack of training, poor communication, or poor work habits. A look at the trending of certain error types can point out areas where additional training or support may be needed. Minor issues, if not made on a regular basis, may not be worth a follow-up unless there is a real trend developing. Forcing responses for every single issue found by a lender's QC department can be costly, create ill will, and lead to a less effective QC process. A better approach may be to identify the frequency of minor issues and their severity, then work only a couple of higher frequency issues each month. By concentrating efforts in this way, a lender can resolve problems rather than create them.

For simplicity of discussion fraud has been divided into three categories: Minor, Major and Scheme.

"Minor" fraud, is fraud that involves only one or two people, even though it is a very serious issue and may be costly, in which some piece or pieces of the income or credit were falsely disclosed and falsely verified. This type of fraud would involve only a single loan transaction. However, this would be an isolated case, not a series of loans. This type of fraud is usually seen as "fraud for property", in which the party really wants to own the home but in actuality cannot afford the payments on their real income.

"Major" fraud is different. These fraud issues must be addressed immediately and responses should be required in a short period of time. These issues come from many sources such as fabrication of the employment by phony companies or in some cases with legitimate companies at false addresses, gift letters, falsification of bank statements, falsification or alteration of checks or money orders, poorly or fraudulently completed appraisals, and title flipping to build a highly inflated value in the property. Assistance in committing some of these acts may unfortunately come from within the lender's own shop. Incentives to produce loans often create incentives to help borrower's qualify even if it takes a "little help". WRONG - such "little help" often leads to bigger help. Hopefully, the major issues are identified and handled without further incidents.

Fraud "schemes" are at an even higher level. A fraud scheme can originate with employees and/or TPOs (Third Party Originators), who are selling loans to multiple wholesale purchasers. Some of these schemes are hard to detect because they are generally more sophisticated and involve multiple players in the process. A scheme usually involves not just the borrower, but the seller, and/or the real estate agent, appraiser, originator, or processor. Schemes go to multiple loan transactions with an ultimate goal of "fraud for profit". This is the worst of all types of transactions to uncover. It can be extremely costly in nature due to the complexity of many schemes and the fact that the

213

loans are disseminated to various wholesale purchasers. It may be some time before the fraud is detected. Once detected it is suggested that the lender investigate immediately to determine the number of loans involved, involvement of common people and other similar characteristics such as gift letters, VOEs (verifications of employment), and VODs(verifications of deposit) to that of the fraudulent loan. It may be necessary to develop a special project or group to review a large percentage of loans where the identified parties are involved to determine the true nature and extent of the scheme. These categories all carry with them intent to defraud the lender and although classified for discussion, they are all serious in nature. Some fraud may be impossible to detect without a discovery of similarities in problem loans or some other intervening fact coming to light.

If a lender encounters fraud, it may be advisable to contact the investor to obtain assistance. Such a contact is a decision left up to the lender's management and, dependent on the nature of the fraud, legal counsel may be needed. Additional contact may be advisable with other lenders who are known to have done business with the same parties. Inter-company contact may determine if additional fraud has been discovered by them and help to determine an approach for pursuit of restitution from, and/or prosecution of the offending parties.

Certain areas of the country seem to be perpetual hotbeds for fraudulent schemes, the west coast, the far southeast, certain areas the northeast and mid-west. These are the more populated areas where the schemes go unnoticed for some period due to the high volume of transactions. It is imperative that a better database of perpetrators be devised by the lending industry which would allow lenders to become aware of potential perpetrators. Although many sources have begun collecting data, there is no single source of such data. No geographic area is immune to fraud and many of the known players move around from area to area boldly perpetrating similar acts at different lenders or different geographic areas.

Often seen as "nit-picky", a good quality control auditor must develop a suspicious nature, good logical, problem solving thought patterns, excellent investigative techniques and communication skills. These traits will help them to detect where problems reside, or may be developing, and communicate with various individuals both within and without the company. The QC department should also be able to provide management with the necessary reports to assess the need for policy changes, additional training, or discipline. The QC professional can provide information needed to request a repurchase of a particular loan by a correspondent, or other provider, when it does not meet the criteria under which the loan was purchased. They may also alert a lender to material or serious defects in loans coming from a particular source or branch thereby allowing time to correct those defects prior to them becoming a marketing or repurchase issue.

High loan-to-value lending brings more people seeking the American dream of home ownership. Lenders and purchasers of loans must adhere to guidelines and be increasingly aware of potential areas of abuse by unqualified borrowers seeking a home they simply cannot afford. Further, an eye must be scanning for criminals seeking profit by defrauding lenders of large sums. In either case, lenders stand to lose and must detect problems that might rob them of their profits or worse. Seeking a quality product is every lender's goal. Investigating suspicious documents in the application process, before the loans are funded, can prevent a loss from being suffered. Beyond that, good post-closing quality control and detailed reporting can help management identify problem areas so they can be dealt with accordingly.

In pushing to move applications through the process to meet the demand for loans, both time and pressure cave in to shortcuts. These cause a failure to closely review certain documents such as gift letters,

215

bank statements, appraisals, or income verifications, to determine their validity. Even worse, there are those within and without the lending community who are aiding, abetting, and profiting from that failure by creating schemes for defrauding lenders or wholesale loan purchasers. It serves lenders well to be vigilant in their efforts to identify abuse and investigate suspicious or potentially fraudulent documents. Some fraudulent documents are so poorly altered or prepared that they can be viewed on their face as being suspect. Misaligned addresses, changes in type fonts, obvious signature mismatches, or missing logos are a few of the common altered documents problems. A quick phone call can be made to determine the validity of the document.

Quality control must be placed in the hands of competent personnel, either internally or with an outsource provider. The quality control department must have access to tools for obtaining information, storing the findings and disseminating the information. A good QC plan must include meeting all of the requirements of the agency or GSE who will be the insurer or purchaser. Their individual requirements are set out in the various investor/agency handbooks or guides. Again, automated underwriting does NOT do away with a need for quality control as it includes representations of data accuracy and data integrity.

Some considerations in building a QC plan:
- Sampling - Select the 10% sample or a valid statistical sample of monthly production. Statistical sampling works only if a lender has a very high loan volume of over 8,000 loans per year. Lenders with less volume should stay with the 10% sampling method.
- Verify the accuracy of information obtained on the loan to determine its validity.

- Review the input and responses on automated underwriting loans for accuracy.
- Identify problems encountered in processing, underwriting and closing the loan.
- Determine the severity of problem issues encountered and the need for a response.
- Report the problem issues and their appropriate severity in summary to management and have backup audit detail available
- Develop a management plan of action to correct the problems and implement that plan.
- A QC plan should allow the lender to obtain and verify the accuracy of the process.
- The QC plan should include the ability to disseminate information to help solve the mystery of: "Who may have done it?". If not, the lender should consider updating the plan and the way it approaches quality control.

If the lender does not have the staff or the expertise for quality control, an option is to look at the advantages of outsourcing pre-funding and/or post-funding quality control. Outsourcing can often relieve a large amount of the effort expended in doing the quality control work and allow the lender's staff time for reviewing issues and implementation of changes that can improve quality. Most outsourcing companies have built sophisticated systems and staffs exclusively for providing quality control services and reports. They should be able to work with a lender to handle customized data, both to and from the lender's system, timely review files to meet agency requirements, customize reports that serve the QC response staff, and provide management summaries that allow upper level management an easy overview of the results. Also, outsourcing makes what would otherwise be a fixed cost vary with the volume of loan production, thus allowing the cost of QC to increase and decrease with the lender's income stream.

Another advantage to outsourcing the quality control function is the objectivity brought to the process by an unrelated third party. In-house audits can create questions about the independence that needs be present in the review and disclosure of process errors and their severity. Outsourcing provides independence, and can also help lenders avoid personality conflicts within their company. The out-source company will look objectively at the file and not involve any conflicting individual personalities in the process.

Pre-funding Quality Control - This is still a relatively new area of quality control. Some steps in the pre-funding process include:

- Re-verifying the existence and address of the employer even if the caller cannot always verify the amount of income paid to the employee. (Sometimes a caller might get lucky and verify actual income.)
- Check to see if the borrower is still employed by the employer given on the application. If not, then where?
- Be certain that the social security number used by the borrower is valid and not being used by others. Be sure to check all co-borrowers as well.
- Use a computerized records check to view the ownership history, how recently the title to the property may have been transferred, and at what reported price.
- An in-file credit report to check any new debts since the original credit check. A bit of diligence here can more than pay for itself if a bad loan is stopped prior to closing and funding.
- If a lender is implementing a pre-funding QC plan, talk with the investors and show them a written plan. The lender may be

pleasantly surprised to find that relief on the post-funding QC requirement is available if a reasonable front-end plan is in place.
- The pre-funding QC plan should have elements that are realistic in relationship to the short time fuse involved in re-verification of application data, usually no longer than 24 to 48 hours.

Quality control can help identify trends where errors are continually made, identify who is making them, and allow the lender to target training to correct those errors. Keeping in mind that quality control only samples the loans produced or purchased by the lender, once issues are identified, it may be necessary to do a larger or targeted sample on the branch, TPO (third party originator), personnel, or service provider where the issues are discovered.

Once the lender has completed the quality control reviews and reports, it is time to work on the responses to issues found. Dealing with issues discovered through the QC audit should be handled based on the severity of each issue, or the regularity of minor issues. Major issues will need to go to specific personnel for response to the findings, while minor issues may be trended and addressed through training, as required. In any event, some method of written response is necessary to clear any major issues discovered. Some lenders may make written memos or notations to or on the QC reports. Others may be more formal and have lengthy responses with exhibits to back up the response. The important thing in QC is to make sure that issues are addressed and all requested responses are in a place available to auditors in the event the lender is called upon to provide them.

Keep in mind throughout the QC process that communication is the key to detecting and correcting quality issues. Good relations and communication between the QC staff, management, and loan production personnel is most important. QC, without any focus or importance placed on it from management, accomplishes very little in making needed changes, either in the loan production process or, if needed, in loan production personnel.

There are side benefits to listening to the QC staff on issues they may encounter in working with the various departments or branches of the lender. QC can advise management on issues regarding loan files being improperly handled and delivered. Lost file and lost document problems can be identified and help a company build a better document management system, speed up shipping, funding, and helping save follow-up cost. Many issues identified through quality control are due to missing documents not being in the file to properly document some aspect of the loan.

A statement that sums it up nicely, "One big loss on a bad loan pays for a whole lot of quality control." Don't share that feeling. It can benefit a lender to pay attention to quality or it can cost the company heavily if it does not.

Technology in Mortgage Originations
by
Mac Russell

In the few years before and after the year 2000, computer technology did more to change the mortgage lending industry than it did in any other period since the inception of lending money. It will continue to play the major role in making mortgage loans easier to obtain with less paperwork, close faster and reducing costs for not only the lender but the borrower as well.

Mortgage lending was one of the first applications for computers, dating back to the 1950's. In the beginning when computers were first used in the mortgage business, they were utilized primarily in the mortgage servicing area to keep track of the loan portfolio, track the payments, and maintain records of escrow accounts for the payment of insurances and taxes.

In the 1980's, computer programs were developed for the origination side of the business and were used to assist the loan officers and loan processors with their paperwork. The programs were very expensive, as was the hardware to run those programs, making automation in the mortgage originations area affordable to mainly the larger mortgage companies. In the 1990's software development companies began to introduce relatively inexpensive programs, that when combined with the faster, more powerful, and lower cost Personal Computer systems, were affordable to just about anyone in the mortgage business. These programs saved a lot of repetitive typing and produced perfect originals for submission to an underwriter for the approval of the loan. It also made it easy to change figures that flow through the entire paperwork system and perform complicated calculations instantly. This was a huge time saver.

In the 1960's, it could take as long as two or three months to obtain a mortgage approval. The process included intensive documentation, such as two or three years of complete tax returns along with W-2's, 1099's, voluminous tax return schedules, pay stubs and bank statements. Written verifications of employment and assets were mailed out to verify income and assets.

Fannie Mae (FNMA - Federal National Mortgage Association) and Freddie Mac (FHLMC - Federal Home Loan Mortgage Corporation), the two Government Sponsored Entities (GSE's) charged with providing funds to purchase home loans, dominate the residential home loan market. They write the rules and guidelines for eligible purchases, and they have also pioneered the way for fast approvals and fast closings. They have, through technology, simplified the entire loan process.

By the late 1990's, Fannie Mae and Freddie Mac had developed sophisticated systems for Automated Underwriting (AU). Many lenders at the time were skeptical that computers and artificial intelligence could replace the long-revered mortgage loan underwriter, the specialist who knew every which way a loan could be approved or denied according to the guidelines established by Fannie and Freddie. But the GSE's proved the skeptics wrong. The advent of FNMA's "Desktop Underwriter" and "Desktop Originator" (known as DU and DO) along with FHLMC's "Loan Prospector" (known as LP) simplified the approval process by utilizing a vast data base of information including credit scores from credit repositories, and valuations from real estate data bases, combined with data from the input file, offering information such as the size of the down payment, liquid assets, time on the job, type of employment, income and type of property being purchased. If the data being input into DU/DO/LP is verifiable, and if the automated response is an approval or accept, a loan applicant can receive an instantaneous commitment and close in a matter of days.

When a loan is submitted to AU, depending upon the quality of the loan itself, credit scores and loan to value being the most highly weighted determining factors, a typical result might require only a pay stub, single month's bank statement and drive-by appraisal. Compare this to the nightmarish scenario described above with the loan approval of the 1960's requiring tax returns, multiple months of bank statements, written verifications of employment and deposits, and an appraisal that requires the appraiser to enter the subject property, measure the rooms, take interior pictures and pictures of the comparable sales used in the determination of value!

Today, a customer can walk into a mortgage lender's office and, after about 20 minutes of providing answers to a loan officer, have an approval directly from Fannie Mae or Freddie Mac. In this instance the loan officer might only need to request an appraisal, now only a three day process, and request title work from the closing agent, which also might only take three days, and this can be going on simultaneously with the appraisal work.

The Internet also plays an important role in the automation process. Desktop Underwriter, Desktop Originator, and Loan Prospector are all Internet based underwriting engines. With no more than a day or two of training a loan officer or processor can become proficient in the use of AU and can gain access to the systems from his/her desktop. Also contained within the Fannie Mae and Freddie Mac web sites are their loan pricing schedules. Most lenders have access to the secured sites that post these prices giving them dynamic pricing and lock-in availability instantaneously. In the case of mortgage brokers and correspondents using major wholesale lenders for their funding, typically the originator will obtain loan approval through DU, DO, or LP and then enter the wholesaler's site for pricing and locking-in. Many wholesale investors email prices to their correspondents and brokers daily with interim updates throughout the day as conditions change.

Businesses that serve the mortgage lending industry have also benefited from advancements in technology. The appraisal industry is one of those areas. Appraisers used to look up comparable sales manually from public records and books produced by the various Boards of Realtors. This was a time consuming, cumbersome process requiring the appraisers to visit the local courthouse to research sales and mortgage recordings. During this process photographs of the property had to be taken and the film dropped off to a photo lab and then picked up a few days later. When the information was finally compiled, manual calculations were performed and then the entire appraisal presentation was manually typed onto the appraisal forms. When the presentation was complete the entire package was put together, with at least one extra copy, and usually mailed out to the lender or mortgage banker/broker. Then if there were any errors in the appraisal, the corrected page had to be retyped and shipped. In most instances fax copies were not acceptable. Technology has provided appraisers with a database of the county records and Real Estate Boards. The appraiser simply needs to define an area and can sort by any number of fields, such as square footage, number of bedrooms, lot size and year built. The photos can be digitally produced, and most of the appraisal presentation can be assembled on the appraiser's computer and emailed to the lender or mortgage broker. If any corrections or revisions need to be made, a corrected copy can be in the hands of the lender in a matter of minutes. It is conceivable that the appraisal will never be printed. It can appear in the lender's loan file as a digital image and can be retransmitted to investors or mortgage insurers without ever having been submitted to paper. Copies can be emailed to the borrower, providing him with a flawless original with color photos. The time frame for doing appraisals has dropped from an average of 10-14 days to 2-3 days. For the same price that appraisals were done in the 1980's appraisers can provide a better quality job with more accurate information in a much shorter time period.

Title work has also been revolutionized due to advances in technology. Not that many years ago title information was derived from enormous volumes called abstracts. In these books was shown the chain of ownership of a property starting with the King of the country who claimed ownership of the property, to the President of the United States at the time the land was deeded, and then all the owners of the property since that time. Abstracts were kept in vaults, either at title companies or in the offices of lenders who held a mortgage on the property. These books were passed on and updated manually by real estate attorneys and title companies at the time of refinancing or sale, and this single event could take weeks. Today most counties have computerized records and the chain of ownership and recorded mortgages are much easier to obtain, making it infinitely easier to produce an updated Title Insurance Commitment or Policy. The county records maintain up to date information about when the title was last updated, so there is no need to continually check the ownership prior to that date.

Prior to the advent of technology even the smallest lender handling only a dozen closings per month either had an in-house document preparation department whose job it was to produce closing documents, or they delegated this task to a closing agent. In either event the process of creating closing documents left itself open to time consuming tedium with every opportunity imaginable to create mistakes. In addition to being susceptible to errors, the document preparation function was slow and could add days to the closing process. Once prepared, the closing package had to be delivered to the closing agent, a step that might also take an extra day or two or three. Added to this was the very real possibility that the package contained an error, which meant starting the entire doc prep process all over again. It was not unusual for a closing to be delayed by days or weeks just on account of the preparation of the closing documents. With modern technology closing packages can be prepared in-house or on-line over the Internet.

Typically the lender will log on to a doc prep service, export the file from the in-house processing system, and create a closing package online. This digital file can be downloaded and printed by the closing agent. Changes can be made instantaneously and new documents can be prepared in minutes instead of days.

Borrowers also have begun to reap the rewards of internet technology in the mortgage banking area. Shopping for interest rates and closing cost scenarios on the Internet is so prevalent that the one of the most telling results has been to cause higher priced lenders/brokers to lower their prices to match the competition. The Internet has dramatically opened doors to the public and made it infinitely easier, in many respects, to shop for a mortgage.

Another difficulty that technology has solved for lenders and mortgage brokers is to help them to be able to determine the exact pricing of a loan taking into account all of the various surcharges that are imposed at loan level pricing. These loan level adjustments are made based upon risk characteristics for various items such as the type of property, the loan to value, the credit scores, the amount of down payment, or the amount of cash out on a refinance. Mortgage lenders and brokers are well aware of the difficulty in quoting a price when one or more of these adjusters is present in a loan scenario. The GSE's and most of the other sources of wholesale mortgage funds have their own schedules of fees for these risk characteristics, but now that so many wholesale sources are posting their prices on the Internet, for a broker or borrower to identify these adjustments has become quite simple. As an example, a non-U.S. citizen purchasing a unit in a hi-rise condominium as an investment, and who wants to make the minimum down payment, will be faced with various fee and interest rate adjustments. This would be a complicated scenario that could take a while to study to arrive at the exact calculations for these price adjustments. But computers can do this in a flash.

Software programs have been developed that take the loan parameters of lenders into a few computer screens that can quickly figure out if the loan can be done, and what the rate and costs will be. This has been expanded into websites where borrowers can input the same information that loan officers do and get the answers to their questions 24 hours a day, 7 days a week. This technology saves countless hours by eliminating a loan that does not fit the parameters. It narrows down the lenders who can provide that unusual niche that a borrower might need. In the past, through the manual process, the loan could make its way all the way to the underwriter only to find out that it could not be approved because it did not meet the lender's criteria.

In development is the electronic signature which is in limited use but is expected to become quite common in the future. Through this technology closings can take place between parties in different cities thus avoiding the awkward and expensive procedure of mail away closings. The day will come when obtaining a mortgage will be as easy and as fast as buying a car.

As time goes on, more and more of the mortgage loan business will be done computer to computer. This has spawned an opportunity for computer programmers in all types of businesses that rely on computers. Virtually all companies must continue to invest in their technology, to update their programs and to add and modify programs in this dynamic environment. The companies that make this investment will reap big dividends later. The good news for the smaller companies and for individuals is that the price of hardware continues to come down as does the cost of the software running on it.

Computer technology is being used more and more frequently to integrate systems within the office to create a more efficient system for both the borrower and the lender. Assuming the phone system is Windows compatible, it can be tied into a contact management system such as Goldmine. When the phone rings, the call is directed to the proper person through voice prompts, and the caller's contact record pops up on the computer monitor. There, right in front of the loan officer or loan processor, is not only the name and phone number of the prospect or client, but his Goldmine record that shows all previous phone calls, any prior loan history, including scanned copies of documents from a prior closing. A dialog box also pops up so that a record of the phone call can be made and attached to the contact record. This way everyone in the office can access the file. This can very useful when a loan prospect says, "I thought you locked in my loan?" A quick look in the history of phone calls might find a notation that provides proof that the applicant declined a lock-in in favor of a float.

Since Fannie Mae and Freddie Mac's roll out of DO/DU/LP, taking the loan application is faster and easier. Numerous software programs for the mortgage industry have been developed and the prices keep falling. Most of the processing software will tie into the various credit bureaus and download the credit history into the loan application, and then tie into the Fannie Mae and Freddie Mac computers and download the pertinent information for an approval. Many of the popular loan processing software packages are priced under $1,000. Through the increased efficiencies of technology, loan officers and processors have doubled or tripled the amount of business they can handle. Loan officers working outside the office can synchronize their notebook/laptop computers in the same manner. This enables a loan officer to not have to come to the main office, saving on office space and staff time. Loan processors no longer have to input the initial loan data because the loan officer will have already done that. This not only increases profits for the lender or mortgage broker, but it allows them to be more competitive due to the economies afforded by these advancements in technology.

The modern loan officer is equipped with a laptop computer that he takes on application interviews. In the presence of the applicant he can run calculations of costs and payments for different loans under different scenarios. To do some of these calculations manually could take a great deal of time. Again, there is software that quickly runs these scenarios and shows the results. In a face to face interview the information can be shown to the applicant right then and there. In the case of a mail or telephone application the information can be emailed to the borrower, and a copy linked to their contact management record.

Another popular use of technology in the mortgage field is a follow up/customer retention program. This software sorts information in its database using parameters as specified by the user. In the context of a mortgage broker, it might be helpful to look for loans originated at interest rates above a certain level or adjustable rate mortgages originated between certain dates. This database can be mined for future contact with a eye toward creating new originations. Often customers will appreciate the fact that their mortgage broker or lender is constantly monitoring their mortgage situation with the idea that if they can improve their terms they will be contacted.

The same tracking software can be used to monitor events that will give the loan officer a reason to contact the borrower. Greetings on birthdays and anniversaries keep the mortgage broker or lender's name in front of the borrower and can set up the basis for having the prospect think in terms of this particular loan officer as being his personal lender. It is an inexpensive marketing tool for the lender/broker and can result in savings to the borrower by dealing with the same company that already has much of the information required to refinance a previously originated loan. It also represents a savings to the lender to retain the servicing rights to the loan.

Computer technology has a very serious side that needs to be considered: security of information. Even the best anti-virus software can be violated. As quickly as a patch is provided for one virus, another pops up. Some hackers are among the smartest programmers in the world. If they can breach the security of the Pentagon, then they surely possess the capability to hack into many other computers. Consider the data that is stored on a computer during the loan process. The record will usually contain not only the borrower's full name, social security number, and date of birth, but it may also contain sensitive bank account information, account numbers, dollar amounts, loan balances, and even related credit card information. This is one of the most important reasons why conscienscious companies go to great lengths to prevent this information from being stolen. There are security measures that should be implemented including encryption, strong password protection, tape back ups, off site storage, alarm systems to the premises, and shredders to destroy sensitive paperwork.

The mother of all nightmares is to have a loan officer's notebook/laptop stolen. Such a computer could contain sensitive information on thousands of customers. Damage from this can be minimized by keeping all of the customer data encrypted with Microsoft's Encrypting File System (EFS). Loan officers are told to log off every time they leave their computers out of sight, even if just for a short time. The theft of the computer is not the problem. Insurance companies would simply reimburse for a newer model, but the real cost is in the compromising of the information within the hard drive. It is the information on the hard drive that is critical.

Valuing a Mortgage Company
by
Michael J. Henry

Valuations of mortgage companies generally occur in conjunction with an effort to sell the subject company. As in any other type of valuation exercise, the objective is to estimate as reliably as possible the future cash flows associated with the business and discount those cash flows back to the present using an appropriate risk-adjusted discount rate. However, owing to the nature of the mortgage industry, this exercise proves to be challenging.

In most manufacturing and service industries, a company progresses through a "normal" cycle of growth, maturity and (perhaps) decline. As a "normal" firm grows, its need for capital grows as well and hopefully, revenues and income grow rapidly until the company reaches the mature stage. During this stage, revenues and income are often fairly flat or gradually increasing. Acquisition and market share issues notwithstanding, revenues and net income can often be predicted fairly easily.

Not so with mortgage companies. Unlike many firms, the fortunes of a mortgage company are directly linked to the interest rate cycle. The refinance wave that began in 2001 is an excellent example of the dramatic growth that ensues in a low-rate environment. During such times, refinances can account for 75% or more of a company's business. However, this can vanish virtually overnight as rates begin to rise. This means that it becomes very difficult to project cash flows beyond six to twelve months and, hence, difficult to produce a reliable set of cash flows with which to estimate value.

As a result, it becomes important for mortgage company analysts to concern themselves with the "quality" of the company's earnings.

This means evaluating both the source and sustainability of the company's earnings. In production companies, this involves analyzing how the company sources loans (i.e., retail, broker, correspondent, consumer direct), the types of product offered (e.g., conforming, government, Alt-A, subprime) and the percentage of refinance vs. purchase business. Finally, monoline vs. traditional business models will greatly affect value. A monoline mortgage company engages in either production (i.e., making mortgage loans) or servicing mortgage loans, but not both. There are virtually no monoline servicers remaining today, due to the scale required to compete effectively as well as the volatility of the servicing asset. There are, however, a great many monoline originators still successfully operating. These companies originate and fund loans, but sell both the actual loan and the right to service that loan. As a result, the originator may collect the first payment or two from the borrower, after which the servicing is transferred to another company.

Traditional mortgage banking companies both originate and retain servicing. This strategy has historically been regarded as wise because of the "natural hedge" afforded by both originating and servicing loans. The idea is that when rates are low, loan production and its related earnings will be high as borrowers pay off high interest mortgages and refinance into lower ones. However, earnings on the servicing portfolio will suffer, because every time a borrower prepays his mortgage, the servicing asset associated with that mortgage vanishes. Conversely, when rates are high, originations and, hence production income will be low because few people will refinance in a high rate environment. Meanwhile, the servicing portfolio will be generating higher earnings because loans are not prepaying. This means that earnings in traditional companies should be smoother than monoline firms as a result of this natural hedge.

The bottom line when valuing a mortgage company is this: **UNDERSTAND THE BUSINESS!** The sustainability of cash flows

232

depends on product type, product source, and management's ability to steer the company through different interest rate cycles. A lack of understanding of the company's history, strategy and business philosophy could result in a serious mis-estimation of corporate value.

Drivers of Value - Production

"Production" refers to the process of making mortgage loans. At various stages through the loan origination process, there are opportunities for profit. The amount of profit an originator realizes depends upon how the loans are sourced, and in how much of the process the originator is involved. The major types of origination "channels" are as follows:

A. Retail - Retail originators are involved in the origination process from beginning to end. The best example is that of a bank branch. The customer fills out an application with a loan officer, a processor inputs, validates and collects any missing data, and an underwriter analyzes the data to determine whether the loan will actually be made. If approved, the bank will fund the loan. Notice that, in this example, no one outside the bank is involved. The bank keeps for itself any application fee, points, underwriting fees and other miscellaneous charges. Additionally, assuming the bank sells the loan and the right to service it, all proceeds from that sale belong to the bank.

B. Wholesale/Broker - Mortgage brokers solicit applications from borrowers and then turn the application over to a mortgage banker for funding. Often, the broker will complete the processing, and sometimes will take part in the underwriting. However, the loan will actually be funded in the name of a mortgage banker. A broker knows how much compensation he will receive from various lenders for providing them with different loan products. When an application is taken, the broker will turn the application over to whomever provides the best price to the broker for that application. For example, the bank referenced above may also purchase loans from brokers. If it does, it will likely split some of the application fee, processing fee and discount points with the broker. It may also give the broker a portion of the proceeds realized when the loan is sold in the secondary market. Clearly, as a result of splitting the revenues, the bank will make less on the loan sourced from the broker as compared to a purely retail origination.

C. Correspondent - While a broker does not actually provide the funds to close loans, a correspondent purchases loans that have already been closed by another mortgage banker. Why? Servicing, for one. A lender with a large servicing portfolio must continue to acquire servicing rights to grow or even maintain the size of its portfolio. Buying a loan "servicing released" means that it is buying both the loan and the right to service the loan. If the correspondent keeps the servicing, it may then either pool the loan with other loans which are subsequently sold and securitized, or it may retain for itself certain loans that it finds attractive. Since many of the revenues associated with the origination process do not flow through to the correspondent, this method of origination has the lowest profit margin.

D. Consumer Direct - This origination channel generally consists of a call center, where sales representatives engage in outbound and/or inbound mortgage loan originations. Such loans are sourced by placing advertisements in print and online, mass mailings and, increasingly, are purchased as leads through companies that source applications from consumers and forward them to banks and other originators who pay for the opportunity to compete for the loan.

In light of the above, one might ask the question: Since retail carries the highest profit margins, why would anyone want to originate through other channels? A primary reason is overhead: a retail platform must lease space, purchase equipment, and hire originators, processors, underwriters, closers, shippers, funders, and quality control personnel. By contrast, much of this expense is either eliminated or reduced through broker or correspondent lending. Given the cyclicality of the industry, it is often those who are nimble enough to downsize quickly who survive. This is much easier to do with a smaller fixed cost structure.

The following table gives a general overview of the profitability differences among the various origination channels. Profitability is expressed below in basis points of production, a common metric of expressing mortgage banking profits. For example, converting from basis points in the chart below and assuming production for the year was $1 billion, pre-tax net income would be $6.0 million for retail, $4.5 million for wholesale, $2.0 million for correspondent and $10 million for consumer direct.

(figures in bps)	Retail	Wholesale	Correspondent	Consumer Direct
Fee Income	100	10	5	100
Gain on Sale	150	150	50	150
Net W/H	20	20	20	20
Total Revenue	270	180	75	270
Expenses	210	135	55	170
Pre-tax Income	60	45	20	100

The second major item to evaluate is the type of product originated. Every product type carries different margins. Product types include conventional (any loan not backed by the FHA or VA), government (loans fully or partially insured by the FHA or VA), Alt-A (loans which do not conform to Fannie Mae/Freddie Mac sale criteria, often because of size or documentation), and sub-prime (loans which are made to borrowers with below-average credit).

Government loans typically carry higher fees than conventional loans. These loans have more paperwork associated with them, and require detailed knowledge of FHA and VA underwriting criteria. The servicing for these loans also fetches a higher premium in the secondary market, as these loans carry higher service fees, provide more ancillary income and generally prepay slower than conventional loans. A summary of the profit margins realized on different product types appears below. The following assumes the loans are originated through a retail channel:

(Figures in BPS)	Conventional	Government	Alt-A/ Subprime
Fee Income	100	125	100
Gain on Sale	125	200	325
Net W/H	20	25	35
Total Revenue	245	350	460
Expenses	200	290	325
Net income	45	60	135

The higher fees for government product are evident. Note also the Gain on Sale. This represents any amount collected upon the sale of a loan in excess of the loan's par value. For example, a $100,000 loan selling for $101,250 would have a gain on sale of $1,250, or 125 basis points. Generally, gain on sale is comprised of servicing value. However, gain on sale also occurs when a loan with an above-current market rate is sold. Notice the 325 basis point gain on sale above for Alt-A/Sub-prime. Because of the lower credit quality, these loans carry higher interest rates. If rates are currently 6% and a mortgage banker sells an 8% loan in the secondary market, that loan will sell for greater than par, all else equal. The servicing value for such loans tends to be lower, however, due to the higher risk of default.

Note also the Net W/H line. This represents net warehouse interest. When a mortgage banker funds a loan at closing, he is typically borrowing 98-99% of the loan amount through a bank line of credit. The remaining 1-2% is funded through the owner's equity retained on

236

the balance sheet. This "warehouse line of credit" provides short-term financing to the mortgage banker, as the loan will be purchased within 30-60 days by an investor (e.g., Fannie Mae, Freddie Mac, or a bank). Therefore, warehouse interest costs are tied to short-term rates. However, most mortgages are priced according to long-term yields. This provides another profit opportunity for the mortgage banker: while the mortgage loan is being carried on the line of credit pending purchase by an investor, the mortgage banker will earn the interest rate spread between the mortgage rate and the warehouse line interest rate (e.g., a 6% loan carried on a line costing 4% in interest nets a 2% annualized spread for the mortgage banker).

Finally, an analyst must consider the company's purchase/refinance ratio. In a "normal" environment, purchases usually account for about 75% of production, while refinances account for 25%. During times of very low rates, this ratio reverses. A heavy concentration in purchase business means that originations will be more stable as rates change. This is because purchase business in the United States tends to remain relatively constant. However, a small rise in rates can cause the refinance market to all but vanish, along with refinance earnings. When rates are low and the 75% purchase/25% refi ratio does not hold, projected originations should be normalized for a more typical interest rate environment. If this is not done, the analyst may well project future earnings that will never materialize.

The most important component of a mortgage banking franchise is its people. Without originators, underwriters, processors and effective management, there are no future earnings. While more qualitative in nature, understanding a company's culture and history can mean the difference between paying a large acquisition premium and none at all.

Which company sounds more attractive?

Company A - Has been operating for ten years. Staff turnover is low and the average tenure of an originator is six years. The staff has been together through both good and bad business environments and has learned how to weather the cycles of the business.

Company B - Has been operating for two years in a low-rate environment. Neither management nor originators have been tested in an adverse business cycle.

Which company would carry a greater value immediately before a market downturn? Analyzing the numbers alone could well lead to similar value estimates; however, the company that would command a franchise premium is clearly Company A.

Finally, the analyst must get a sense of the company's "story". Almost every company has one. Perhaps it has established a network of relationships with builders, developers and Realtors, thereby contributing to a strong purchase mix of business. Maybe it has unsurpassed customer service, or maybe it has an expertise in generating a niche product line. In any case, understand what makes the company different. Ultimately, the buyer of a production franchise is faced with a fundamental decision: to build a franchise de novo or buy an existing one. A company needs to be able to convince a potential acquirer that it offers that unique "something" that cannot be easily replicated and, therefore, commands a premium.

To summarize, the following are five important considerations in assessing a company's production franchise:

- Channel Mix
- Product Mix
- Purchase/Refinance Ratio
- People
- A Unique "Story"

Once the analyst understands the above, he can confidently anticipate the company's future success in changing environments.

Drivers of value - Servicing

When a mortgage is originated, the lender has to choose between selling the mortgage in the secondary market and retaining the mortgage on its own balance sheet. The overwhelming majority of mortgages originated in the United States are sold in the secondary market.

When a mortgage loan is made, two distinct assets are created: the loan itself and the right to service that loan. Mortgage servicing is the process of collecting a borrower's monthly payment and remitting that payment to the appropriate parties (usually securities investors, property tax collectors, and insurance companies). It also involves processing loans that pay off before they are contractually due and administering the default process when a loan becomes delinquent and goes into foreclosure. Often when loans are sold, the loan itself is sold to one party (the "investor") and the mortgage servicing right (MSR) to another. The purchaser of the MSR must estimate the net present value of the cash flows associated with servicing the loan and carry that amount on its balance sheet as an asset, with amortization being booked throughout the expected life of the MSR.

For companies actively involved in loan servicing, this asset often constitutes the largest piece of the company's value. Therefore, the ability to accurately calculate the market value of MSR's is extremely important.

Like any other financial asset, valuing mortgage servicing involves estimating the revenues, expenses, and net cash flows associated with the asset over its expected life. These future cash flows are then discounted back to the present using an appropriate risk-adjusted discount rate. Following is a brief description of the major revenue and expense line items associated with mortgage servicing:

Revenues:

Service Fees - While a mortgage servicer collects the entire payment due from a borrower, it will not pass through this total payment to the investor. Rather, the servicer will retain a portion of the interest, usually about 25 basis points (1/4 %) for conventional loans and 44 basis points for government loans.

Escrow/Float Earnings - The servicer must remit the payments it receives to the investor on a specific day each month. This means the servicer can earn interest income on these funds until it remits them to the investor. The number of days of float varies by investor. Additionally, borrowers often escrow their property taxes and homeowner's insurance. Once again, the servicer may be allowed to earn interest income on these funds until they must be remitted to tax collectors and insurance companies. Servicers often have this cash on hand for several months. For practical purposes, instead of receiving actual interest on these escrow and float funds, the servicer often receives a credit that reduces other fees in its banking relationship.

Ancillary Income - The servicer collects the contractual late fee when a borrower becomes delinquent on their payment. Also, fees are charged for miscellaneous services such as providing payoff quotes and amortization schedules.

Expenses:

Servicing Cost - Mortgage servicing is an industry that is heavily reliant on both people and technology. Call centers are staffed with customer service personnel to answer customer questions, as well as a myriad of other staff functions: investor accounting, payment and payoff processing, new loan set-up, default management, information systems, and executive management. In addition, the servicer must lease its office space, pay utilities, buy office supplies and license various servicing software applications. Due to the many fixed costs as well as the expense involved in acquiring cutting-edge technology, achieving scale is important in the servicing business. The servicing cost per loan for a small servicer can easily be three times that of one of the largest.

Interest on Escrow - In some states, servicers are required to remit a portion of the escrow float earnings described above to the borrower. That partial payout of float earnings to the borrower is an expense. However, the servicer still generally earns a spread over the interest amount paid to the borrower.

Advance Costs - Servicers are sometimes obligated to make full payment of principal and interest to an investor whether the borrower actually makes their payment or not. When the borrower does not pay, the servicer must advance this amount to the investor out of its pocket. Funds to make advances are generally acquired through a bank line of credit, which carries an interest cost to the servicer. Also, the servicer will pay property taxes and insurance payments even if there is not enough cash in the borrower's escrow account to do so. This is because the servicer wishes to preserve its position as first in line to foreclose in the event the borrower defaults. If property taxes go unpaid, the first priority position goes to the taxing authority.

Default Costs - Even though a very small percentage of loans are ever actually foreclosed (about 1%), administering the default process can be complex and costly. While FHA and VA loans reimburse the majority of the servicer's default expenses, other loan types do not offer such protection (although the loan may carry private mortgage insurance, which does mitigate default risk). The servicer must follow a prescribed method of customer communication in an effort to bring the loan current. Failing that, the servicer maintains the property through the date of foreclosure sale, which is often twelve months or more. In order to estimate all of these cash flows to conduct a valuation of the servicing rights, several assumptions must be made about the future behavior of the portfolio. The most important are:

Assumptions:

Prepayment Speed - Most loans do not exist through their contractual maturity date. They are refinanced for a lower rate, borrowers trade up, are relocated, or for one of many other reasons pay off before the loan fully amortizes. Therefore, it is vitally important to estimate as accurately as possible the rate at which loans will pay off early. This is best achieved by observing past prepayment tendencies in a similar environment. There are many commercially available services which use complex mathematical functions to estimate prepayment speed. Bloomberg L.P. also surveys Wall Street dealers twice monthly to obtain the prepay speed of the mortgages underlying the bonds that these companies sell. These "Bloomberg Median" speeds are widely used in the industry to estimate prepayments.

Earnings Rates - Float and escrow earnings depend on the rate at which the servicer can invest those proceeds. The market generally assumes a five-year swap rate or LIBOR-based rate to estimate these earnings.

Discount Rate - Cash flows must be discounted at the appropriate risk-adjusted rate of return in order to be valued properly. This rate is dependent both upon the general interest rate climate as well as the loan type. The more liquid and easy to service, the lower the discount rate. For example, loans in Fannie Mae pools are discounted at a lower rate than loans in Ginnie Mae pools, due to differences in servicing complexity, asset liquidity and delinquency statistics between these loan types.

Servicing Cost - As described above, actual servicing cost can vary widely. However, in the marketplace, bidders assume a marginal cost to service in estimating cash flows, as opposed to a fully loaded cost (i.e., the servicer doesn't need to build another building or hire another executive vice president to service one additional loan). In general, cost to service is estimated at $40 - $60 per loan per year, with conventional loans on the low end of this range and government loans on the high end.

Ancillary Income - Generally, analysts assume $30 - $40 of ancillary income per loan annually, with conventional loans at the low end and government loans at the high end.

Below is a sample valuation output for a servicing portfolio. For this example, a portfolio of 70,000 mortgage loans, with a combined total unpaid principal balance of $10 billion, was used. While this may sound like a large portfolio, it is actually quite small, as some portfolios literally contain millions of loans.

Using one of the many commercially available MSR valuation models, along with current market assumptions for servicing yields, a set of cash flows associated with the above portfolio is created. While different models may produce somewhat different results, valuation results should all be within a range of 2-3 basis points of unpaid principal balance. Following are projected cash flows for the first 12 months of the sample portfolio:

REVENUES

Month	Servicing Income	P&I Float	T&I Float	Late Charges	Prepay. Float	Total Revenue
1	2,083,333	72,504	361,733	158,652	324,491	3,000,714
2	2,046,567	71,315	356,533	16,5050	318,761	2,949,226
3	2,010,432	70,145	351,408	153,491	313,131	2,898,607
4	1,974,919	68,995	346,356	150,973	307,597	2,848,840
5	1,940,017	67,863	341,377	148,497	302,158	2,799,913
6	1,905,716	66,750	336,470	146,062	296,813	2,751,811
7	1,872,006	65,655	331,633	143,666	291,560	2,704,520
8	1,838,876	64,578	326,865	141,310	286,398	2,658,027
9	1,806,317	63,519	322,166	138,992	281,325	2,612,319
10	1,774,319	62,477	317,535	136,712	276,339	2,567,382
11	1,742,872	61,453	312,970	134,470	271,439	2,523,204
12	1,711,968	60,445	308,471	132,264	266,623	2,479,772

EXPENSES

Month	Servicing Cost	Advances	Foreclosure Cost	Interest Lost	IOE	Total Expenses
1	262,500	4,753	14,583	136,507	105,484	523,827
2	258,726	4,675	14,344	134,096	103,968	515,810
3	255,007	4,598	14,109	131,728	102,473	507,915
4	251,341	4,523	13,877	129,400	101,000	500,142
5	247,728	4,449	13,650	127,112	99,548	492,487
6	244,167	4,376	13,426	124,863	98,117	484,949
7	240,657	4,304	13,206	122,654	96,707	477,527
8	237,197	4,233	12,989	120,482	95,317	470,218
9	233,787	4,164	12,776	118,348	93,946	463,021
10	230,427	4,096	12,567	116,250	92,596	455,935
11	227,114	4,028	12,360	114,,189	91,265	447,957
12	223,849	3,962	12,158	112,163	89,953	442,085

INCOME/VALUE

Month	Net Income	P/V of Cash Flow
1	2,476,887	2,459,163
2	2,433,416	2,398,715
3	2,390,691	2,339,736
4	2,348,699	2,282,190
5	2,307,426	2,226,042
6	2,266,862	2,171,260
7	2,226,993	2,117,809
8	2,187,809	2,065,658
9	2,149,298	2,014,776
10	2,111,448	1,965,131
11	2,074,248	1,916,695
12	2,037,687	1,869,437

The cash flows shown above would continue through the expected life of the portfolio, usually 300+ months. However, the bulk of the value is derived from the first 4-5 years of cash flow, due to the effect of discounting. For this portfolio, the resulting value is as shown below:

VALUATION OUTPUT

Value of Servicing in $	$98,412,273
Value of Servicing as % of UPB	0.984%
Servicing Multiple	3.94

Note that value can be expressed in three different ways: in total dollars, as a percentage of UPB ($98,412,273/$10,MMM = 0.984%) and as a multiple of the portfolio's weighted average service fee (0.984/0.25 = 3.94).

Example of Mortgage Company Financials

Financial statements for mortgage companies have many similarities among firms. While line items may be categorized and grouped differently, all mortgage banking operations have largely the same cash inflows and outflows. Following are a sample balance sheet and income statement for a fictitious mortgage banking firm. It is assumed that this company retains and manages a servicing portfolio. If this company sold all of its loans servicing-released, the line items related to mortgage servicing would not appear on the company's financial statements.

The largest asset on the Jones Mortgage Company balance sheet is Loans Held for Sale. This represents loans that the company has already made to borrowers. At this stage, the company owns the loans. In order to disburse funds to close the loan with the borrower, the company borrowed on its warehouse line of credit with its bank. The bank holds the mortgage note as collateral until the mortgage company pays back the advance. This occurs when an investor buys the loan. Generally, loans will remain in the warehouse line for 30-60 days pending purchase by the investor. Note the corresponding liability, Warehouse Loan Payable, which is $12 million dollars less than the

Loans Held for Sale asset. This $12 million is funded by the mortgage company itself.

Portfolio Loans are often assets that the mortgage company has sold and subsequently repurchased. An investor may require a mortgage company to repurchase a loan because of an underwriting deficiency discovered after the loan was sold, if fraud exists, or if the loan becomes delinquent early in its life. Upon repurchase, the company may deem it more beneficial to hold and service the loan on its own balance sheet instead of selling it at a deep discount to another investor or, in the case of a defaulted loan, foreclosing.

The Servicing Rights asset refers to the projected net present value of the company's mortgage servicing portfolio. In this case, it is assumed the company owns a portfolio identical to the one used in the servicing valuation example. The value of this asset will be amortized annually according to its expected life. Occasionally, a servicing portfolio's market value will fall more quickly than its planned amortization suggests. This occurs most often when mortgage rates are declining and prepayments increase, thereby reducing the size and value of the servicing portfolio. In these cases, a special "impairment" charge is taken.

Jones Mortgage Company
Balance Sheet
($ in 000's)

Assets

Cash	$ 30,000
Loans held for Sale	620,000
Portfolio Loans	4,000
Servicing Rights (net)	98,412
Accrued Interest Receivable	2,000
Premises and Equipment	5,000
Other Assets	10,000
Total Assets	**769,412**

Liabilities

Warehouse Loan Payable	$	608,000
Note Payable- Building		5,000
Accrued Payroll		6,000
Other Liabilities		20,000
Total Liabilities		**639,000**
Equity Capital		**130,412**
Total Liabilities and Equity Capital		**769,412**

Accrued Interest Receivable represents interest owed to the company on loans currently held in its warehouse line. The company will often collect the first payment or two even if it is selling the right to service the loan. The income statement is presented in segmented form; that is, production profitability and servicing profitability are shown separately, then summed to show total corporate profit. Various items such as occupancy and administrative expenses are allocated as corporate overhead on a pro-rata basis according to the amount of each resource used by production and servicing. Note also that the production income statement is presented both in actual dollars as well as in basis points of production volume. Evaluating an income statement in terms of basis points allows for easy comparison between companies of different sizes, and makes it much simpler to identify operational strengths and weaknesses between firms or as compared to industry averages. Likewise, the servicing income statement is shown in actual dollars and dollars per loan, which is the common metric used in comparing different servicing operations.

The first items shown on the income statement are Interest Income and Interest Expense. Interest Income refers to interest collected on mortgage loans while they are in the warehouse line. Interest Expense refers to the interest paid to the bank and is the cost of financing loans in the line. As discussed earlier in the chapter, in most yield curve environments the difference between interest collected and paid is positive and therefore a revenue source to the mortgage company.

Jones Mortgage Company
Segment Income Statement
($ in 000's)

Origination Volume	$8,000,000		Loans Serviced		70,000
Revenues	*Production*	*BPS*	*Servicing*	*$/Loan*	*Total*
Warehouse Interest Income	$ 62,000	78	$ -		$ 62,000
Warehouse Interest Expense	(38,000)	(48)	0		(38,000)
Net Warehouse Spread	$ 24,000	30	$ -		$ 24,000
Net Gain on Sale of Mortgage Loans	$ 80,000	100	$ -		$ 80,000
Processing & Underwriting Fees	8,000	10	-		8,000
Mortgage Servicing Revenue	-	-	33,000	471	33,000
Total Revenue	$ 112,000	140	$ 33,000	$ 471	$145,000
Expenses					
Commissions	$ 40,000	50	$ -	-	$ 40,000
Servicing Salaries	-	-	3,000	43	3,000
Payroll & Benefits	3,000	4	1,000	14	4,000
Direct Loan Costs	2,000	3	-	-	2,000
Occupancy	1,000	1	2,500	36	3,500
Amortization of MSR's	-	-	11,000	157	11,000
Repurchase/Indemnification Provision	1,000	1	-	-	1,000
General & Administrative	5,000	6	5,000	71	10,000
Total Expenses	$ 52,000	65	$ 22,500	$ 321	$ 74,500
Income Before Taxes	$ 60,000	75	$ 10,500	$ 150	$ 70,500
Taxes	24,000	30	4,200	60	28,200
Net Income	$ 36,000	45	$ 6,300	$ 90	$ 42,300

Net Gain on Sale of Mortgage Loans refers to the price received for loans in excess of par value in the secondary market (i.e., from investors). This represents payment for premium loans with coupon rates above par at the time the loan is locked with the investor. In the case of loans sold servicing released, it also includes the value of the servicing right being sold with the loan. Discount points collected from the borrower may also be included in the gain on sale. If a loan was sourced through a broker, the broker will often receive a portion of the gain on sale. Hence, "net" gain on sale represents the gain after any broker commissions are paid. Mortgage Servicing Revenue represents the actual revenues of the servicing portfolio. This includes servicing fees, float income, and ancillary income. Commissions represent compensation to loan officers for originating mortgages. Direct loan costs generally relate to appraisal fees, survey fees, etc. that can be directly attributable to specific loans. As mentioned earlier, the MSR portfolio is being amortized by $12 million per year. A Repurchase/ Indemnification provision is also shown. This is a reserve to fund the occasional loan repurchase request from an investor.

Valuation Technique

Thus far, the value drivers of mortgage production franchises as well as the valuation methodology for servicing portfolios have been discussed in detail. The final task is to bring this information together and look at the corporate valuation process itself.

In valuing any company, it is wise to approach the valuation process from several different angles. Doing so will enable the analyst to better identify any misspecifications in the valuation assumptions as compared to using a single method. In general, there are three approaches used to value mortgage production companies. In each method, the goal is the same: to estimate as accurately as possible the expected future economic benefit (i.e., cash flow) that a buyer of the company would be likely to realize. Future cash flows are estimated by conducting a servicing valuation (as described above) and by forecasting the present value of cash flows from mortgage origination activities. The sum of these two components represents the expected future cash flows.

However, to run a business, capital must also be invested to secure a warehouse line, lease office space and furniture, and provide for everyday expenses. The seller has built that capital through its initial equity investment and by retaining a portion of earnings through the years. Since this capital (aka net worth, equity or book value) represents the seller's investment in the company, the seller expects to have this investment returned, along with a premium, upon sale of the company. Putting these components together, then, results in the following general formula for the value of a mortgage company:

> ## Total Value = Market Value of Servicing + Origination Franchise Value + Seller's Equity

The three approaches to value mentioned above include:

1. *Net Present Value* - This is the most theoretically correct way to value a series of future cash flows. In this case, the expected future cash flows associated with the production franchise are estimated, and then discounted back to the present using an appropriate risk-adjusted discount rate. As discussed earlier, the challenge is in correctly identifying the future cash flows, since the fortunes of mortgage companies are so heavily dependent on interest rates.

2. *Production Premium* - This approach looks at past production volume, estimates future "normalized" volume, and assigns a premium according to the channel mix of the originator.

3. *Market Multiples* - This method seeks to find publicly traded companies that bear a strong resemblance to the company being valued (seldom an easy task). Then observed Price to Earnings (P/E) multiples of the public companies are applied to the subject company's projected earnings to arrive at a value estimate.

It should be emphasized that P/E ratios already capture the net worth of the company. By contrast, production premiums and NPV of future earnings approaches do not include corporate book value, which must be added separately.

As an example, below is a valuation model for the hypothetical Jones Mortgage Company described above.

Seller's Equity Value: A prospective purchaser will presumably be acquiring the balance sheet of the company. This means that, upon closing, the purchaser will own the company's assets and take responsibility for the company's liabilities. The difference between assets and liabilities is the company's equity. As mentioned above, the seller expects to receive its book value at closing. However, the purchaser will

	Low	High
Servicing Value	93,400,000	103,400,000
Tangible Equity	27,100,000	32,000,000
Production Premium	32,000,000	64,000,000
Total Value	**152,500,000**	**199,400,000**
Book Value	130,412,000	130,412,000
Premium to Book Value	**22,088,000**	**68,988,000**

Therefore, the estimate of total company value is a range of $153 - $199 million. Of this, $130 million represents the company's book net worth, leaving a premium above book value of $22 - $69 million.

P/E Comparison:

As a final check, assume that the following three publically traded companies were identified as being close comparables to the Jones Mortgage Company. Assume all have production as well as servicing and originate primarily conventional, broker/correspondent product. The companies forward P/E's (i.e., P/Es based on forecasted 12-month earnings, as opposed to past 12-month earnings) are as follows:

Jones Mortgage Company Projected 12 month earnings: $38 million

	Forward P/E	Implied Value (Jones)
New York Mortgage Company	4.9X	$ 186,200,000
Miami Mortgage Company	4.2X	$ 159,600,000
Buffalo Mortgage Company	5.3X	$ 201,400,000

	Low	High
Implied Value Range	$159,600,000	$201,400,000

Applying these observed multiples to Jones' estimated earnings of $38 million results in the Implied Value Range. This range based on P/E's can be compared to the range developed above as a "reality check". As is often the case, the P/E's of the publicly traded companies in our example imply a higher value than our other valuation methods. This is largely attributable to the size and share liquidity of the publicly traded firm as compared to the smaller, privately held company.

In any case, it is easy to see that the final value range is fairly wide! There is a $47 million difference between the low and high ends of the range in these examples. What, then, is the appropriate value? While only hindsight will eventually tell, it comes down to the intangibles mentioned earlier:

- Can past volume and profitability be replicated?
- How strong is the management team?
- Does the staff work well together?
- What has turnover experience been?
- What is the perception of the company in the market place?
- What does your gut tell you?

Transaction structure also significantly affects the ultimate price paid. Total deal consideration is often broken up into two parts: the closing, or non-contingent payment, and the contingent payment. Typically, a payment is made at closing equal to the company's book value plus a portion of the premium. The remainder is paid out depending upon future performance. If the seller is willing to take a larger percentage of the sale price in the form of a contingent "earn-out", the ultimate price received may be toward the higher end of the value range. Alternatively, if the seller chooses to take the entire payment up front, it can count on receiving significantly less.

Finally, look to the market to gauge the level of comparable corporate transactions that have recently occurred. If nothing else, this will give a good indication of what the seller may be expecting to receive! Making certain to consider all of the factors discussed in this chapter, qualitative as well as quantitative, will help to assure an accretive transaction.

Glossary

Glossary

Adjustable Rate Mortgage: A mortgage that permits the lender to make periodic changes to the interest rate.

Amortization: The gradual repayment of the balance of a mortgage through periodic, usually monthly, installments of principal.

Amortization Schedule: A timetable of payments for a mortgage that shows the amount of each payment and the application of principal and interest, and the remaining balance of the loan.

Annual Percentage Rate: The total cost of mortgage financing expressed as a yearly rate that includes interest and certain closing costs paid by the borrower.

Appraisal: A professional opinion as to the value of a property.

Appreciation: An increase in the value of a property.

Assumable Mortgage: A mortgage that can be taken over by the buyer of a property

Assumption: The transfer of a mortgage from the seller of a property to the buyer.

Balloon Mortgage: A loan that requires the payment of the remaining principal balance fo the loan all at once before the loan is fully amortized.

Binder: A preliminary agreement that sets forth the basic terms of understanding. A binder can precede a sales agreement between a purchaser and seller, or may represent the promise of an insurance company to issue a policy for title or hazard insurance.

Cap: A provision of an Adjustable Rate Mortgage limiting the amount by which interest rate or payments may increase or decrease.

Clear Title: Title to a property that is free of encumbrances or questions of ownership.

Closing: Also known as "settlement" or "escrow". A meeting or ceremony at which the sale of a property is consummated by the seller delivering a deed to the buyer and the buyer delivering the cash to close and/or executing mortgage documents.

Closing Costs: Expenses related to a closing ahat are over and above the price of the property. Examples of closing costs include title insurance, homeowners insurance, lender's points, appraisal fees, documentary stamps and inspection fees.

Commitment Letter: A formal offer by a lender stating the terms under which it agrees to provide funding to a borrower.

Condominium: A form of property ownership in which the homeowner holds title to an individual dwelling unit of a multi-unit project in addition to an interest in common areas and use of certain limited common areas.

Conforming Loans: Loans that fall within the dollar limits and underwriting guidelines of Fannie Mae, Freddie Mac, FHA or VA.

Conventional Mortgage: A loan that is not insured by the Federal Housing Administration or guaranteed by the Veterans Administration.

Convertible Adjustable Rate Mortgage: AN Adjustable Rate Mortgage that can be converted to a Fixed Rate Mortgage.

Cosigner: A person who agrees to assist a primary borrower by guaranteeing the loan.

Covenant: A clause in an agreement or declaration that restricts a borrower or property owner and which, if violated, may result in a default.

Credit Report: A report of an individual's credit history prepared by a credit bureau or consumer credit reporting agency. Credit reports are used by lenders to determine a borrower's creditworthiness.

Debt-to-Income Ratio: A measurement of a borrower's overall ability to service his total monthly obligations. The ratio is derived by dividing the total amount of monthly obligations including credit card installments, auto payments, housing expense and all other monthly obligations extending beyond ten months, by the borrower's monthly gross income. In the instance of FHA insured mortgages, net income is used.

Deed: An instrument conveying title to property to another person.

Deed of Trust: The document used in some states instead of a mortgage. Property is transferred to a trustee by the borrower and then reconveyed when the debt is paid in full.

Default: Failure to make mortgage payments in a timely manner or to comply with other requirements of a mortgage.

Deferred Payment Loans: Any loan where repayment is scheduled at a later date such as a Reverse Mortgage.

Delinquency: The period in which scheduled payment is past due but not yet a default status.

Depreciation: A decline in property value.

Down Payment: The part of the purchase price that the buyer pays in cash and does not finance with a mortgage.

Due-on-Sale-Clause: A provision of a mortgage that permits the lender to require payment in full upon the transfer of title to the mortgaged property. Sometimes referred to as an *Alienation Clause*.

Earnest Money: A deposit given with an offer to purchase property as evidence that the buyer is serious or committed to the sale.

Easement: A right of way granted by the owner of a property giving others access to or across the property.

11th District Cost of Funds (COFI): An index that tracks the weighted average cost of borrowings and savings for member banks of the 11th District of the Federal Home Loan Bank Board which includes California, Arizona and Nevada. This is a popular index for use with Adjustable Rate Mortgages.

Encumbrance: A claim or lien attached to the title to a property.

Equal Credit Opportunity Act (ECOA): A federal law that prohibits lenders from considering race, gender, age or marital status in the granting of credit.

Equity: A homeowner's financial interest in the property. The value of the property less the amount of mortgages outstanding.

Escrow: The holding of money or documents in a real estate transaction by a neutral third party (the escrow agent) prior to a closing.

Also, an account held by a mortgage servicer into which moneys are deposited for the payment of real estate taxes and insurance.

Fair Credit Reporting Act: A consumer protection law that regulates the disclosure of consumer credit reports and establishes procedures for correcting mistakes in a credit record.

Federal Home Loan Mortgage Corporation: (FHLMC or Freddie Mac) A secondary mortgage market corporation chartered by the federal government whose function it is to create liquidity and an orderly market for the sale of home loans in addition to establishing underwriting guidelines for conforming mortgage loans.

Federal Housing Administration (FHA): An agency of the U.S. government (under the U.S. Department of Housing and Urban Development; H.U.D.) that insures residential and multifamily mortgages.

Federal National Mortgage Association (FNMA or Fannie Mae): A secondary mortgage market corporation chartered by the federal government whose function is to create liquidity and an orderly market for the sale of home loans in addition to establishing underwriting guidelines for conforming mortgage loans.

First Mortgage: A mortgage that is in first position on the title to a property and has first claim against the property in the event of a default.

Fixed Rate Mortgage: A mortgage in which the interest rate remains the same throughout the life of the loan.

Flood Insurance: Insurance that protects a homeowner and/or lender in the event of damage by flooding. Flood insurance is a federally subsidized program and is intended for properties in designated flood areas.

Foreclosure: The legal process by which a lender acts to take title to a property on account of a default under the mortgage indebtedness.

Graduated Payment Mortgage: An adjustable or fixed rate mortgage in which the payments increase according to a predetermined formula for a specified period of time.

Hazard Insurance: Insurance coverage that compensates the owner and /or lender for physical damage to a property.

Home Equity: A homeowner's financial interest in the property. The value of the property less the amount of mortgages outstanding.

Home Equity Loan: A loan secured by the owner's equity in the property. Most often a junior lien to a first mortgage.

Homeowners' Insurance: Insurance coverage that compensates the owner and/or lender for physical damage to a property. Homeowner's insurance policies often have riders that cover other losses such as theft and liability.

Homeowner's Warranty: A guarantee or insurance that covers repairs to specified parts of a home for a specified period of time. Homeowner's Warranties are usually given by home builders.

HUD 1 Statement: See Settlement Statement.

Index: A published measurement of certain interest rate movements or averages that result in a number by which adjustments to adjustable rate mortgages are calculated.

Interest Rate: The percentage of an amount of money that is charged for its use usually expressed as an annual percentage.

Jumbo Loan: AL loan with a balance that exceeds the limits permitted by Fannie Mae and Freddie Mac.

Loan Servicing: The collection of mortgage payments from borrowers along with the related responsibilities such as principal and interest passthrough to investors, payment of escrow items and investor accounting.

Late Charge: The penalty a borrower pays when an installment payment is received after the due date.

Lien: A legal claim or encumbrance against a property that must be paid or assumed before title can be transferred.

Lifetime Cap: The limit that an interest rate pr payment rate can reach at any time during the life of an adjustable rate mortgage.

Loan-to-Value Ratio: The relationship between the loan amount and the lower of the purchase price or appraised value, where the loan amount is divided by the value.

Lock-in: A written agreement from a lender guaranteeing an interest rate to a borrower provided the loan closes within a specified period of time.

London Interbank Offered Rate: (LIBOR): A popular index for establishing interest rate changes to adjustable rate mortgages.

Maturity: The point at which a loan becomes due and payable either through amortization or a balloon payment.

Mortgage: A legal document that pledges a property to a lender as security for payment of a debt.

Mortgage Banker: An individual or company that originates and funds, and sometimes services, mortgage loans.

Mortgage Broker: An individual or company that arranges mortgage financing for a borrower with a lender for a fee.

Mortgage Insurance: See Private Mortgage Insurance.

Mortgage Insurance Premium: The fee paid by a borrower to the FHA or mortgage insurer for mortgage insurance.

Mortgage Margin: The amount that is added to an index to calculate the interest rate in an adjustable rate mortgage.

Mortgagee: The lender in a mortgage transaction.

Mortgagor: The borrowing entity in a mortgage transaction.

Negative Amortization: An increase in the principal balance of a mortgage obligation which is created as a result of a payment rate lower than the amount needed to service the debt based upon principal balance, interest rate and term. Deferred interest and/or principal payments result in negative amortization.

Notice of Default: An official notification from a mortgage lender or servicer to a borrower that a default has occurred and that legal action may be initiated.

O.C.C.: Office of the Comptroller of the Currency- The federal agency that regulates commercial banks.

O.T.S.: Office of Thrift Supervision-The federal agency that regulates Savings Banks and Savings and Loan Associations.

Origination: The administrative process of creating a mortgage, including document verification, document preparation, closing and funding.

Origination Fee: A fee charged by a lender or mortgage broker for arranging a loan. Origination fees are usually expressed as a percentage of the loan amount.

Owner Financing: A purchase transaction where the seller of the property provides some or all of the financing to the buyer.

PITI: The monthly payment combining principal, interest, taxes and insurance.

Points: Fees charged by a lender or mortgage broker for originating a loan. One point is equal to one percent of the loan amount.

Prepaids: Expenses in a closing transaction that are prorated and paid in advance to set the loan up on the lender's books. Prepaid items include interest, real estate taxes and insurance premiums.

Prepayment: The payment of an additional amount of principal on a mortgage over and above the scheduled amount.

Prepayment Penalty: A fee that may be charged to a borrower for paying off all or part of the principal balance of a mortgage in advance of the scheduled payment.

Prequalification: An informal process used to determine how much an applicant can borrow based upon unverified information provided.

Preapproval: A formal process, more binding than a prequalification, in which a lender states how much money they will lend based upon the information the have verified.

Principal: The amount owed on a loan.

Private Mortgage Insurance (PMI): Insurance provided by a non government entity that protects the lender in the event of a default.

Purchase and Sale Agreement: A written contract between a buyer and seller binding each other to the sale of a property subject to the terms of the agreement.

Qualifying Ratios: Guidelines established by a lender to determine the maximum loan to grant to an applicant.

REO (Real Estate Owned): Property acquired by a lender through default of the borrower through foreclosure or deed.

Radon: A colorless, odorless gas found in some homes that can cause sickness if present in sufficient quantities.

Real Estate Settlement and Procedures Act (RESPA): A federal law that protects the borrowers by requiring lenders to disclose closing costs in advance of a settlement.

Real Estate Taxes: Yearly tax assessed on real property.

Refinance: Paying off one loan with the proceeds of another loan using the same property as collateral.

Reverse Mortgage: A mortgage loan that enables elderly homeowners to take advances against the equity in their home either in lump sums or installments with usually no obligation to repay until the property is sold.

Second Mortgage: A mortgage in lien position subordinate to a first mortgage.

Secondary Mortgage Market: The institutional market place where closed mortgages are bought and sold.

Settlement: See "closing".

Settlement Statement (HUD1): A document that evidences the sum of all costs and amounts due to and from the buyer and seller in a real estate transaction.

Survey: A map or drawing of a property showing precisely where the boundaries are along with the locations of buildings, easements, rights-of-way and encroachments.

Teaser Rate: An attractively low interest rate, usually in an adjustable rate mortgage, that acts as an initial start rate, but is not necessarily in alignment with the market for interest rates on similar mortgages that have already had their first rate adjustment.

Term: The length in years of a mortgage obligation.

Title: A legal document evidencing a person's ownership if a property.

Title Company: A company that examines and insures title to property.

Title Insurance: An insurance policy that insures a lender or buyer against loss arising from disputes over ownership.

Title Search: An examination of the public records to determine the condition of the title to a property.

Treasury Bill (T-bills): Short term U.S. government securities. The interest rates on various Treasury Bills are used as indices for the changes to adjustable rate mortgages.

Truth in Lending Act: A Federal Law requiring lenders to disclose the terms and conditions of a mortgage including APR and other charges.

Underwriting: The process of evaluating a loan application to measure the risk associated with the granting of credit. It involves verification and examination of credit, income, cash reserves, and property characteristics and value.

VA Loans: Loans guaranteed by the Veterans Administration.

ACKNOWLEDGMENTS

This project could never have come together had it not been for the contributions of some of the best minds that I have ever met in Mortgage Banking and related professions. I thank each of them for the time they have taken to create these chapters, and for their diligent efforts to convey messages of vital interest and importance to anyone who intends to finance a home or to learn more about how that is done. And to all of the people who have supported and assisted these contributors, another special thanks.

A few of the contributors also want to acknowledge others for their assistance:

Don Rosenthal acknowledges the contribution of the Mortgage Insurance Corporation Association (MICA) for its excellent treatise on the Private Mortgage Insurance industry and how Private Mortgage Insurance works. This important chapter tells the complete story of an industry that might be the single most important enhancement to home finance since the invention of the thirty year fixed rate mortgage.

Michael Henry knows as much about valuing a mortgage banking company and mortgage servicing rights as anyone I have ever known. His excellent chapter, *Valuing a Mortgage Company*, is something every Mortgage Banker and their CPAs should read. Mike was brought to the group by Jeffery Levine of Coral Gables, Florida, and who works with Mike at Milestone Partners. Jeff was instrumental in giving technical advice for the chapter.

Paul Hammond of Studio 41 in Boca Raton must be recognized for his creativity in designing the graphics for the cover work. Everything Paul touches becomes a work of art.

PROVIDERS FINANCIAL INC.
2420 WEST VISTA WAY
SUITE 102
OCEANSIDE, CA. 92054